To Kathy

When A Man's Fancy Turns To Cooking

G. Wesley Rice

6/7/96

G. Wesley Rice

Ponca City, Oklahoma

PecanQuest
Publications
Ponca City, Oklahoma

On the Cover

Upper Left - Morel Mushrooms. After the confines of winter, a man's fancy often turns to the outdoors. A favorite pastime after the first sizable rain in spring is to seek the morel mushroom. Morels are found over much of the USA, and are fairly unique in appearance. There is little danger in mistaking them for something else. Besides breaking a spell of cabin fever, morel hunting provides superb table fare.

Upper right - Truchas, New Mexico. A picturesque village at the edge of the Española Valley, and sheltered by the Truchas Peaks, the Truchas area inspired much of my interest in New Mexico Cuisine. I had a superb view of the Truchas Peaks from my office window in Los Alamos, New Mexico. Nearby is the village of Chimayó, location of the famous Rancho de Chimayó Restaurant.

Lower left - Herbs and Spices. Perhaps the most unique feature of this book is the collection of herbal blends used in recipes throughout the book's pages. The book offers nine herbal blends used for chicken, bean, Mexican dishes, and others.

- SPICE ISLANDS® is a registered trademark of Specialty Brands, Inc.

- *Schilling*®, and *McCormick*®, are registered trademarks of McCormick & Company, Inc.

Other referenced commercial manufacturers and products include : Lea & Perrins, Honeysuckle White®, Salman Ranch, Tabasco®, Libby's®, Jiffy, Kraft Miracle Whip®, and Pace®. The author expresses his appreciation to these manufacturers and many others for their quality products.

Library of Congress registration in progress

Printed by : Ag Press, Inc.
Manhattan, Kansas

This book is dedicated to my wonderful family - my wife, children, brothers, and sisters. They taught me much about the art, science, and luck of cooking. They enjoyed the successes, and didn't complain about the failures. In memory of our parents, now departed, and other family members who now seek that special recipe in a better place.

Acknowledgments

Most of the recipes in this book are the result of experimentation with ingredients and proportions. Of course, all cooks that I know have referenced recipes from many sources. We add a little of this, and vary seasonings and other ingredients. This is the gift of creativity. I voice my thanks and appreciation to the multitude of individuals who have written down both processes and ingredients in a multitude of cookbooks, providing both joy and sustenance to humanity (and probably a dog or two).

My wife, Margaret, has included a selection of recipes that was passed down through her family's generations. These were passed in person from her paternal grandmother, Florence Johnson. Florence was of Swedish ancestry. We are unsure of the specific authors of these recipes.

Photographs

All photographs were provided by the author. I express my appreciation to **Drug Warehouse**, and **Photo•pro** - both of Ponca City, Oklahoma, for their assistance with special processing.

Illustrations

- Illustrations on pages 77 and 96 were drawn by my sister, Geneva Davis from Wildorado, Texas.
- Illustration on page 70 was drawn by my daughter, Jeanette Kite from Arkansas City, Kansas.
- Other illustrations were drawn by the author.

Important Note: Herbal Blends

Many of the recipes in this book call for at least one of my nine special herbal and spice blends, such as *Rice's Chicken Enhancer™*. **The recipes for these blends are found on pages 21-23.** I find it convenient to make batches of these blends, and store in containers for future use. This avoids getting all the herb and spice containers down when you cook.

Table of Contents

The above contents include recipe origins and human interest observations. For a special list and corresponding page numbers of these *non-recipe* items, see the section following the index.

Wild blackberries make excellent jellies, jams, cobblers, and more. If the seeds bother you, process the berries through a sieve, or colander.

Sand plums, and other wild plums make superb jelly. I've eaten sand plums straight off the tree. Wasps love plum thickets, so beware!

Elderberry bushes provide both edible blossoms and fruit. Blossoms can be harvested in late spring; fruit is ready in the late summer.

Poke is preferred by many over spinach and other "tame" greens. Some parts of the plant are poisonous. Avoid using berries, roots, and stems. Always prepare the leaves according to directions - page 35.

Lamb's quarters sustained many people during the depression, and is a green still favored by many. Use some in bean dishes.

Like the morel, puff-balls are easily recognized edible mushrooms. This picture illustrates the Western Giant Puff-ball in a New Mexico rural setting. Always cook puff-balls soon after gathering, while the interior is pure white. As with all edible mushrooms, eat only a little the first time you try one.

Plantain is a green that is common over most of the USA. While young and tender, it is a tasty addition to salads. Plantain is also acceptable as a cooked green prepared like spinach.

Wild garlic is widespread in distribution, and is usually unmistakable due to the distinctive odor. Use in place of tame garlic in a variety of dishes. Avoid eating similar looking plants that don't have a garlic or onion odor.

Wild native pecans and black walnuts are delicacies that can be eaten right out of the shell, or used in a host of recipes. Each native tree is a variety of its own, so search for the ones that have the best properties, such as easy cracking and shelling.

Peppers are the mainstay of many Mexican foods, such as the fresh red salsa shown at the right. A blend of peppers provides a more robust flavor than any single variety. Vary the proportions to adjust the degree of "fire". Recipe on page 86.

Chiles have tough skins, and must be peeled before using. Place chiles over hot charcoal or under a broiler to blister the skins, then place peppers in a plastic bag and cool quickly. See page 79.

Pecans and black walnuts enhance many foods, such as choco-nutaholic cookies shown at the right. Shelling ease of wild pecans and black walnuts varies significantly from tree to tree. Recipe on page 100.

Spinach salad is both wholesome and colorful. This rendition uses a hot dressing. Recipe on page 58.

Herbal Steak Diane uses the author's Beef Enhancer in addition to the traditional seasonings. Recipe on page 59.

Chile rellenos are a little tricky, but well worth the effort. Choose straight, thick walled Anaheim or other long green chiles. Poblano peppers are also used for this tasty dish. Serve with either a tomato sauce or a queso sauce. Recipe on page 92.

Krukräkers are an unusual Swedish dish and a potato lovers delight. Don't expect a perfect rendition the first time you make them. Recipe on page 122.

Tortilla soup is my favorite soup recipe. The recipe has chicken, cheese, tortillas, nine vegetables, plus herbs and spices - certainly a full, well balanced meal. Recipe on page 64.

Smoked brisket. Perhaps the secret of an exceptional brisket is in the marinade. Recipe and procedures are on pages 112 and 114.

Chapter 1

Introduction

Throughout history, cooking was traditionally part of woman's domain. On different occasions though, man dabbled in the culinary arts. There were and still are, of course, some fine male chefs around. We see them in restaurants, on TV, and elsewhere. Back in my younger days, most of the cooks in the neighborhood were women. Looking through church and other cookbooks, I see more recipes authored by women than men - lots more as a matter of fact. As a paper carrier, it was always the women who provided me with homemade cookies and such; I don't remember a single instance of goodies provided by the men-folks of the family. In those days it was even safe to trick-or-treat for things not adorned with sealed wrappers.

There are exceptions to every rule though. Even in those earlier days, some cooking chores were often chalked up as man's domain. Take the barbecue grill for instance. I think I saw more men out in the yard by the barbecue grill then; the same holds true today. The smell of wood smoke must be more becoming on a man than a woman. Chefs from the unfairer sex also abound at certain "male" activities. Women aren't often invited on hunting and fishing trips, and other male "hen" parties-- or I guess I should say rooster parties.

I'm also a big fan of western novels. If those western novels were truthful, most of the chuck wagon bosses were men. Chuck wagon menu items usually weren't very imaginative. Typical fare included beef, beans, coffee, sourdough biscuits, and an occasional can of peaches. Maybe this is why the cowboys couldn't wait to return to civilization and partake of woman cooked vittles.

In my own family, my wife and I shared the cooking chores, although when the kids were growing up, Margaret had the primary cooking responsibility. I was lucky enough to cook more or less when and what I wanted. In those days, men were often the sole breadwinners. This was especially true when the kids were too young to look after themselves. Later, when my wife decided to practice her profession as a teacher, the cooking load became more balanced.

Another difference in those older days was the eating-out syndrome. During the World War II days, and several years thereafter, eating out in our neighborhood was virtually nonexistent. When I got my paper route at age 11, I did splurge occasionally to visit the Lotaburger® stand. If I recall correctly, burgers cost about a quarter and French fries cost a dime. I was in high school when I had my first full-fledged restaurant prepared steak dinner. All those salad dressing choices were a mystery.

As described in the next chapter, I always did like to cook. My flair was for the unusual; some might even say for the complex. The pages of this book describe things that I enjoy cooking most. These pages also provide some background information on different cooking styles, where some of the recipes come from, and so on. The book also describes food know-how that is hard to come by. For example, the book describes wild edibles and their preparation.

Selecting and pre-preparing ingredients is especially important. Please take special care in this important step. The best spices, superb cooking know-how, and other expert steps can't make good food out of poor ingredients. Once good ingredients are selected and properly pre-prepared, **herbal and spice blends** often make the difference between good and superb. Many of my favorites are listed on pages 21-22.

Although my book relates to man's fancy in cooking, women, I'm sure, can do a marvelous job with these same recipes and cooking styles. So this book, although written from a man's perspective, can hopefully be enjoyed by all.

Chapter 2

<u>Origins</u>

Cooking always interested me. My memories of this particular obsession of mankind date back to about first grade. I started school during the middle of World War II. Like most people, my childhood memories of earlier times are kind of fuzzy. It's hard to sort out actual experiences from the ones constructed in the mind from hearing the tales of others.

Food memories in my early years are also fuzzy to non-existent. I know that I must have eaten something because I grew bigger and stronger. I don't remember having the aversion to green vegetables that my grandsons have -- but maybe I did. Mention spinach, broccoli, and other such stuff and they turn as green as the vegetables. Come to think of it, broccoli must have been invented in the 1950's.

As the youngest of five children in our family, I had not experienced the great depression. My mind does have pictures of these depression days though. I can visualize the milk cow staked out on the vacant lots; the lamb's quarters picked from a cultivated weed bed. Real vegetables took too much water to be practical. These and other stories told by my brothers and sisters are almost as if I had experienced them. Perhaps profound experiences are also inherited.

In my early days, food must have always been there when I was hungry. We were one of the luckier - or maybe I should say more fortunate nations during the late 1930's and early forties. Other countries caught up in World War II didn't have things as good. Oh, we had some minor inconveniences such as ration stamps and scarce items. Sugar, flour, and other staples sometimes ran out before the recipes that called for them did. Improvising and creativity were important. Trips to the grocery store were staged with care since gasoline was rationed as well. Sometimes the shelves that held that needed item were bare.

I also draw a blank when trying to recollect what food dishes adorned our table during the early war days. I remember the green beans and potatoes from the garden. Then there were the white patty-pan squash. Dad always liked patty-pans better than the more common yellow variety. I can picture them in the garden, but not in the food bowl. I can remember lard and the container of bacon grease that was always on the stove. Mom dipped into it from time to time as a seasoning. When it was full, the bacon grease container contributed to lye soap. I don't recall even hearing the word cholesterol.

Fast food hadn't been invented back in those days either. Eating out was almost nonexistent then, at least in our neighborhood. There were, of course, no special kids meals with the memorable toys. Our grandchildren retain memories of the toys and forget the food specifics. The first time I remember eating out was soon after the war. We went to a fried chicken restaurant. Some relatives from Oregon had been visiting and wanted mom to get a reprieve from the kitchen. I remember that I was shocked that my relatives left a whole dollar tip.

Mom, with help from my sisters, provided three meals a day, regular as clockwork. Cooking was a requirement - not something done for fun. In my grade school days, I remember the smell of cabbage cooking; the smell of homemade sauerkraut in that special crock; the wild ducks that she parboiled before placing them in the oven. I remember the Irish stew, meat loaf, pot roast, and fried chicken on Sunday. Chickens came from the yard and not from the grocery store. Then there was that special kitchen stool that dad made. I pulled it regularly to the kitchen sink - or counter as it was called. The stool gave me that added height to see what mom was doing. No fancy mix-masters; no blenders; no food processors. Instead there was the potato masher, the eggbeater, and the cheese grater. Things were done by hand.

I also remember the pancakes. I watched from the stool the standard round ones -- and sometimes a special form that simulated a rabbit, turtle, or other critter. Somehow, those animal forms always tasted better than the round ones. I remember the special book of the tiger being chased until it turned to butter. My, how good that butter must have tasted.

That unique kitchen stool is still one of my most treasured possessions. Today, my grandsons love to watch my pancakes form in the shape of tractors, dinosaurs, and so on. They say that the round ones aren't nearly as good.

Our meals in my early days were plain by today's standards. I can even remember some of the basic contents. There were fresh vegetables in the summer. When the garden was bare, the vegetables came from grocery store cans and canning jars that mom had filled from the garden. Meats consisted of staple cuts of beef and pork from the grocery store, and the occasional chicken from the yard. Fish were usually ones that were caught from City Lake or Buffalo Lake. Of course we grew up in an environment that might be rated as poverty level today. We supplemented things from the grocery store with a victory garden, fresh eggs from the chicken yard, and meat from the chickens. Hunting and fishing were always favorite pastimes; not so much for sport but for supplemental table fare. Cottontail rabbits were plentiful and close by. Amarillo was on a major flyway, so wild duck and an occasional goose often found its way to our table. Catfish were in a nearby lake that was in striking distance of a bicycle. During the war, gas was too scarce to use the car for these purposes.

Hamburger (ground beef) was a staple. I'm sure we had hamburgers for lunch maybe twice a week. My two sisters were at home, along with the younger of my two brothers -- at least until he went to Japan a few weeks before V-J Day. My older brother was in the armed services since the war's beginning. Dad left for the ordinance plant early in the morning and came home late.

Thus we homebuddies (homebodies?) got kind of creative with our limited ingredients. Maybe the missing family members who were deprived of eating these creations were really the lucky ones. We concocted hamburger enhancer that was appropriately named *ooey-gooey*. It was made by browning onions in the hamburger grease, then adding catsup and mustard and some other stuff. The "other stuff" was our individualized personalized secret ingredients. Each family member cook took turns to try and out do the others. We slapped *ooey-gooey* on the bread or buns (can't remember which) along with the hamburger patty. Maybe we should have patented the formulas because if memories don't lie, it often outdid McDonalds®. Some of the older folks ruined the whole episode by including such yuk things as lettuce and tomatoes. My brother even added raw cucumbers from time to time-- can you imagine! Pickles, maybe -- but not cucumbers. I wasn't a fan of tomatoes and lettuce then. Must be some kind of a built in mechanism since my grandkids think the same way. Our three children were also inflicted with this early dislike for healthy things as I remember.

A vivid memory that comes to mind often was the ice delivery man. Refrigerators were yet to replace iceboxes in our neighborhood. Old Tally (Tall-E, not Tally as in bridge score pads) we called him. He had to stoop to clear the seven foot front door header. He usually turned up his nose at our culinary arts. One day, I guess he was especially hungry because he asked for a sample. I was the cook of the day. Kids even in those days could be kind of mean. I guess I was no exception. I had picked some especially hot peppers out of my Amarillo garden -- and Amarillo can grow some really fiery peppers. My special *ooey-gooey* formulation had included a smidgen of this hot stuff. Maybe it was only a half smidgen, come to think of it. I put the rest of the batch in Tally's burger. Good thing he was an ice man.

Soup was also on the menu often. Sometimes it came from a can. Other times mom or my sisters made it from scratch, or maybe I should say from what was available. My brother was more of a breakfast cook and didn't mess around with the complex world of cooking lunch and dinner. I think we called these meals dinner and supper back then.

I guess I learned from some of these early exposures to basic cooking. The importance of good soup bones, browning some things, not browning other things, chicken broth, fresh vegetables, the wonders of certain peppers, and more were instilled at an early age. I can't remember when I cooked my first entire meal, but I do remember many dishes prepared in my junior high and high school days. I was an *ooey-gooey* expert by the age of eight.

Cooking changed from a chore to an enjoyable experience sometime about junior high age. I discovered that foods could be made to taste better if special seasonings and other ingredients were added. Oh, there were the occasional highlights earlier, such as tricking ole Tally, the iceman. Junior high was when I entered the culinary experiment stage. While mom used basic salt and black pepper, I was more creative.

Gardening was a favorite pastime, and I was fascinated with herbs. I was on a first name basis with basil, oregano, sage, rosemary, and others. Herbs and other flavor items such as peppers made my cooking different than the family standard. My sisters were married and off on their own. My brothers were back from the war, working, and attending college. Mom and dad caught the brunt of my experimentation. I usually tasted it myself ahead of time to issue any warnings that were necessary.

Peppers also fascinated me. I started first with the standard bell peppers. They grew pretty well in my Amarillo garden. I graduated from bell peppers to banana peppers; then to some of the more exotic varieties such as Hungarian wax and Jalapenos. This was before the days of the milder Tam Jalapenos. Regular Jalapenos were a little too hot for my taste buds. Pepper plants are pretty and fun to grow. Bugs don't appear to be fond of pepper plants. Maybe the plants, like the fruit, burn the eyes and mouths of the insect critters. My introduction to Anaheim and the New Mexico chiles was to come later. I found that blends of these peppers changed the flavor of some of my dishes substantially. My first tendency was to overdo it. If a little of my pepper blend helped; a bunch would be super. Right? Wrong! Too much peppery stuff, like too many cooks, spoil the broth.

We had one cookbook as I remember; cookbooks cost money. There was a little information on using herbs, and even less on using peppers. Most of my enhanced dishes resulted by trial and error. Ingredients also cost money, so we ate all the trials and all the errors. Mom and dad kind of shied away from these "enhanced" flavors at first, but later grew to like them. Mom was even caught up in the herborama and used a few from time to time. Brothers and sisters even invited me over to fix a few meals. They liked the cooking but hated my mess. I learned that somebody else's mess always looks worse than your own.

I never was too picky about the kind of fish I ate, because fishing was a favorite pastime. We always ate what we caught. I got to be a master with the filet knife. Even the tiniest bluegills were turned into wonderful boneless morsels. They were dredged in flour and cornmeal, then cooked in bacon grease. I can't specifically remember when cooking oil came on the scene. I remember the white shortening, and even the white oleo - with the yellow color tablets. The Government must not have wanted us to mistake oleo for butter. Lemon juice, homemade tartar sauce, and other flavor enhancers came later to my seafood world.

In the Texas Panhandle, catfish came in two flavors- channel cats and mudcats (bullheads by proper nomenclature). My newly acquired sister-in-law liked channel cats, but despised mudcats. Maybe it was the name or the terminology. Mudcat doesn't sound too appetizing. I never could tell much difference in the overall taste. I had also become somewhat of a catfish guru. Mudcats themselves even came in several different flavors. The brown bullhead was cleaner looking, and had whiter flesh that the darker skinned varieties. My secret was to filet the mudcats, cut out the dark lateral line, and soak the resulting fillets in a little lemon juice and salt water. This made the fillets even whiter.

I sneaked a little of my specially prepared mudcat into the channel cat dinner. You know, my sister-in-law gobbled down that ole mudcat like it was the best thing ever. Then of course, maybe she was just trying to be nice. I learned one valuable lesson though. Initial care and processing of the basic ingredients correlate highly with the quality of the final food product. The old saying, "garbage in, garbage out" applies especially in preparing foods.

Thus some of my best dishes had their origins in these early days. I learned both what to do and what not to do. Cooking, like many things, never reaches perfection. New things come along. Tastes and attitudes change; thus do recipes. Like decor, some foods are the rage for a while -- then disappear. Some are, however, tried and true. They may undergo variation and modification to some extent, but the identity never changes. Vegetable soup will always be vegetable soup. Chili will always be chili. barbecue, chicken and dumplings, ... and so on. My versions of these special recipes have been personally modified over the years. They have stood the test of time. Things have been added; other ingredients have been removed. These are the *creme-de-la-creme* of my culinary advances.

In some ways, I hate big cookbooks. It takes time to hunt through the chaff to find the wheat, so to speak. Thus, I've selected just a few of my best recipes. Remember, good cooking takes time, at least in my opinion. Most of these dishes can't be whipped-up in five minutes. Many have basic collections of ingredients that are common, and can be prepared ahead of time. They can even be frozen for later use. I've arrived at some common herbal blends, and herb-spice combinations. These I often mix in bulk, and reference as a single item. Don't leave out the "trace elements." They make the difference between good and superb. The key to most of these recipes is the stock. I have a chicken stock, a beef stock, an Italian stock, three NuMex stocks (sauces), and a easy to make roux that are used extensively in my recipes. These stocks can be prepared in bulk and frozen in zipper plastic bags until ready to use.

Another requirement is proper preparation of ingredients. Take chicken for example. I always, **always,** soak my chicken in ice water and salt for at least an hour. Then, I rinse it off and put it in a zipper plastic bag and refrigerate until ready to use. Just before it's used, I rinse it again. Blood is removed with these steps, making the chicken whiter and better tasting. So with this nostalgia behind, let's look at some basic herbal and spice blends, stocks, and recipes.

<u>Notes</u>

Chapter 3

Herbs and Spices

Many of my recipes call for half a dozen or more herbs and/or spices. I got tired of getting all those jars and containers out every time I wanted to make chili, vegetable soup, chicken and noodles, and so on. Genius comes slowly to some of us, I guess. Why not make up a big batch of these herb and spice blends, and dish out the right amount for the recipe? One jar; one measuring spoon. No more tiny amounts of "trace element" herbs that might evaporate when they fall from the measuring spoon to the pan. So that's what I did.

The following blends are used in many of the recipes that follow. They can also stimulate your creativity. Use them for dishes that I've never thought of. You can even think up some of your own. Let me know if you come up with something super-tasty.

Many of the blends are listed in "parts", where a part can be any measure that you want. For example, if you want a big bunch of the stuff - a cup can be the unit of measure. If you want a small bunch of the stuff - use a teaspoon. Other blends use a mixture of units. Of course, you can always double or half the recipe. Keep a calculator handy.

Oh! One other word. I like real live garlic instead of garlic powder or salt --or even the ground real stuff that comes in jars. In some cases, however, I do use garlic powder in the herb-spice blends to supplement the real garlic in recipes.

Herbs and spices are thus the basis for unique flavor and aroma for many dishes that would otherwise be plain by anybody's standards. They yield a uniqueness that makes much of the difference between Chinese, Mexican, and other foods. The use of herbs and spices can also be overdone. Start with a little, then add sparingly.

Herb-Spice Blends

Certain herbs naturally enhance certain foods. Rosemary, for example, is almost always associated with pork and lamb. Sage is always associated with stuffing, but it also adds a touch of spice to pork, fowl, and so on. Thyme is the time-chosen herb for almost everything, especially tomato dishes.

NuMex and TexMex cooking uses various forms of peppers, although peppers aren't really herbs. Ground red chile is properly classified as a vegetable. Cumin, anise, and oregano are common herb-like cooking ingredients. The coriander/cilantro plant produces both leaves and seeds that are used in Mexican dishes. Cilantro is typically referenced as the leaves, while the seeds are usually referenced as coriander (usually ground).

Tarragon is often associated with seafood; basil with Italian food; saffron and turmeric with Middle East countries; and so on. Get to know the different herbs and spices by their smell and taste. Don't be embarrassed if you use something that isn't traditional. Foods are in the tastes of their beholders. If a herb appeals to you and your family, use it.

Herbal blends, like music notes, provide a unique harmony in the end product. By varying the combinations and amounts, an almost infinite range in tastes and aromas can be constructed from a dozen or so herbs and spices. The following blends are some of my favorites. Don't be afraid to experiment. These blends were arrived at by trial and error. Maybe you'll find some that you like better.

The blends assume dried products. Fresh herbs always add a unique touch when they are available. Sometimes the flavor varies between a fresh herb and its dried counterpart. As a rule of thumb, use about four times as much fresh product as dried. As I said before, amounts are specified in units. Depending on desired quantity, a unit can vary from a cup down to a teaspoon. Use the same measure for each ingredient. Starting out, a teaspoon might be a good choice.

> "Herbal blends, like music notes, provide a unique harmony in the end product."

Blend 1 (*Rice's Tomato Enhancer* ™)

1. 6 units of thyme
2. 2 units of oregano
3. 1 unit of dill leaves
4. 1 unit of basil
5. 1 unit of cilantro (optional)
6. 1 unit parsley
7. 1 unit chervil
8. bay leaves (remove before serving)

> Add one bay leaf for each tsp. of the mixture.

Blend 2 (*Rice's Chicken Enhancer*™)

1. 3 units of thyme
2. 2 units of oregano
3. 1 unit of marjoram
4. 1 unit of rubbed or ground sage
5. 1 unit of cilantro
6. 1 unit of ground rosemary
7. 1 unit of tarragon

Blend 3 (*Rice's Beef Enhancer*™)

1. 2 units of basil
2. 1 unit of rosemary
3. 2 units of oregano
4. 1 unit chervil (parsley can be substituted)

Blend 4 (*Rice's Pork Enhancer*™)

1. 2 units sage
2. 2 units rosemary
3. 1 unit chervil
4. 1 unit oregano
5. 1 unit tarragon

Blend 5 (*Rice's Seafood Enhancer™*)

1. 1 unit tarragon
2. 1 unit rosemary
3. 1 unit sugar or brown sugar
4. 2 units onion powder
5. 1 unit garlic powder
6. 2 units lemon pepper
7. 1 unit cilantro leaves
8. 2 units paprika

Blend 6 (*Rice's Bean Enhancer™*)

1. 3 units of thyme
2. 1 unit of sage
3. 2 units of oregano
4. 2 units of chervil (parsley can be substituted)
5. 1 unit of cilantro

Blend 7 (*Rice's Red Herbal Chili Blend™*)

1. 1 cup chili powder
2. ½ tsp. sage
3. 6 Tbs. cumin
4. 5 tsp. sugar
5. 3 Tbs. paprika
6. 1 tsp. black pepper
7. 3 tsp. oregano
8. 2 tsp. dried cilantro
9. 3 tsp. garlic powder
10. ½ tsp. coriander
11. 2 tsp. salt
12. ½ tsp. marjoram
13. ½ tsp. thyme

Makes enough for 10 pounds of meat; 2 pounds of meat requires 5 Tbs. mix.

Blend 8 (*Rice's Green Chile Blend™*)

1. 6 units of cumin
2. 6 units of white pepper
3. 1 unit ground cloves
4. 1 unit sage
5. 2 units coriander
6. 2 units cilantro leaves
7. 4 units of oregano
8. 2 units salt
9. 2 units sugar
10. 2 units garlic powder

> This blend is typically used as an additive to dishes that call for green chile. It is also useful where the color or flavor of red chile seems inappropriate.

Blend 9 (*Rice's Molé Blend™*)

1. 1 unit salt
2. 2 units cinnamon
3. 1 unit coriander
4. 1 unit cilantro leaves

> **pronounced moh-lay**

5. 6 units Pasilla red chile powder (preferred)
   or 4 units regular red chile powder
6. 1 unit ground cloves
7. 1 unit nutmeg
8. 1 unit anise (omit if you don't like licorice)
9. 1 unit allspice
10. 1 unit white pepper

Notes

Chapter 4

<u>Stocks and Sauces</u>

These are not the stocks as in "stocks and bonds", but are the liquids that are a constituent of some of my favorite dishes. A properly prepared stock can be the secret of your success; a poor stock can ruin your meal. Use fresh ingredients. Throw those old shriveled carrots and other whimpy and discolored veggies in the trash and not in the stock pot!

One of my pet peeves is to have chicken and noodles served to me on a plate, with a fork as my only weapon of attack. In my opinion, good chicken and noodles needs to be served in a bowl, with lots of that good juice. A spoon is essential for eating it properly, although a fork may come in handy too.

I have several stocks that are the basis for many of my dishes. With good stocks, you can be creative. You can make tasty meals with the veggies and meats that you like. I use basic chicken stock for lots of things -- from chicken and dumplings to bean soup. Each stock does have its place though. A roux based stock, for example, is typically reserved for gumbo.

In my opinion, pre-preparation of recipe ingredients, the stocks, and their close relatives--sauces and marinades--are the keys to good cooking.

Chicken Stock

Pre- preparation

Select a fryer-broiler about 3.5 pounds in size. Remove giblet package, and split the chicken lengthwise down the back, leaving the breast intact. You can also use about 3.5 pounds of fryer-broiler parts. Backs, wings, legs, thighs, or any combination of bony parts will do. Clean the dark organs from inside the back, ribs, etc. These dark items will discolor the stock if left on the chicken. Soak the chicken in cold salt water for about an hour or longer, adding ice cubes if necessary to keep the chicken cold. Rinse the chicken and use immediately, or store for up to a day in the refrigerator. If stored, rinse the chicken again before using. If not used in a day's time, freeze the chicken for future use.

Ingredients

1. Prepared chicken (soaked in salt water and rinsed)
2. 1 large stalk celery or celery base (stem end)
3. ½ cup onion or outer layers to approximate ½ cup
4. 2 cloves garlic
5. 1 tsp. salt
6. 2½-3 quarts of water (or enough to cover the chicken)
7. 1 medium potato, pared

Blender liquefy potato in two cups of the water. Place chicken and other ingredients in a large pot/dutch oven. Simmer for about two hours, or until chicken separates from the bone easily -- but not too easily. Overcooked chicken is more difficult to work with than just-right chicken. Remove chicken from the stock and set aside to cool. Strain the chicken broth through a mesh strainer, or for super clear stock place a paper towel or coffee filter in the bottom of the strainer, and pour the stock through. Do in two or three batches to avoid excessive clogging. Use or freeze in zipper plastic bags. Separate chicken from bones and skin; save or freeze for future use.

Beef Stock

The secret to good stock is a good bone(s). Select shin or shank bones and have your butcher cut them in about one to three inch slices. Use about one pound of bones for 4 cups of stock. Soup bones are better if they have a little meat attached.

Ingredients (for 8 cups of stock)

1. 2 pounds of soup bones
2. 1 stalk of celery
3. ½ cup onion
4. 2 cloves garlic
5. 3 quarts (12 cups) water
6. One potato, pared and quartered (optional)
7. 1 Tbs. Worcestershire sauce
8. 2 bay leaves
9. 1 tsp. salt
10. 1 Tbs. cooking oil

Heat a stock pot at medium high heat until a drop of water sizzles. Brown the bones best as you can in the oil. Turn the heat to low, cover, and cook the bones with no water added for about 20 minutes - shaking occasionally. Add water and all other ingredients and cook covered for at least 2 hours. Discard bones and vegetables. Strain the stock. Use immediately, or freeze in zipper plastic bags. I find 4 cups to a quart bag convenient.

NuMex Stocks/Sauces -- See NuMex Section -- pages 82-87.

"The secret to a good stock is a good bone"

by: Wes Rice

KATIE

27

Italian Sauce

When tomatoes are abundant in the summer, Italian sauce is an effective way to use the excess. Place **ripe** tomatoes in boiling water for a minute or so, and then place them in cold water. Skins will slip easily. Remove skins, cores, and any blemishes. Wash the innards of prepared tomatoes to remove as many seeds as possible. The recipe makes a pretty big batch (about 5 quarts). The sauce freezes very well, and makes excellent spaghetti sauce. Puree the sauce for excellent pizza.

Ingredients

1. 12 cups prepared chopped fresh tomatoes. 12 cups (about 6 cans) of canned tomatoes can be substituted.
2. 2 cups of chopped onion
3. ½ cup minced celery
4. ¼ cup minced garlic
5. 3 chopped banana peppers, seeded and peeled
6. 4 bay leaves
7. 1 Tbs. chopped fresh parsley or cilantro (I like cilantro)
8. 3 Tbs. *Tomato Enhancer*
9. 3 Tbs. fresh basil--chopped, or 2 tsp. dried basil
10. 2 Tbs. olive oil
11. 2 Tbs. sugar
12. 3 cups tomato sauce (three 8 oz. cans)
13. 12 oz. tomato paste (one medium can)
14. 2 tsp. salt

Cook onion and celery in olive oil over medium heat for about 4 minutes, or until the onion is translucent. Add all other ingredients and simmer slowly for about 3 hours. Stir occasionally to avoid sticking. **Remove bay leaves**. For a smooth sauce, puree in a blender or food processor until the sauce takes on a desired consistency. For a chunky sauce, use as is. For a meaty sauce, add one pound of cooked ground beef to one quart of sauce.

Roux (easy, reduced fat)

One of my favorite seafood dishes is a good gumbo. Gumbo is also one of the worst dishes to concoct, partly because of the roux that's required. Conventional roux calls for browning flour in fat in a skillet. Getting it right is tough! Too much cooking burns the mixture. Also, it's far easier to create lumps that resemble tough brown dumplings than to get a smooth roux. It's also easier to get a pale anemic looking roux than a brown just-the-right-color roux.

So much for how not to make roux. This recipe calls for browning the flour in an oven. Less guesswork, probably fewer burned fingers, easier cleanup, and the results are comparable to the tough way of doing things. Use in gumbos, beans, other soups.

Ingredients

1. ½ cup flour
2. 1 Tbs. Worcestershire sauce
3. 4 or 5 shakes Tabasco® sauce
4. 1 medium onion, quartered
5. ½ cup green or banana pepper, chopped into large pieces
6. 1 tsp. salt
7. 6 cups chicken stock

Place flour in a 9*9 pan. Shake until flour is evenly distributed. Place in an oven preheated to 375° . Cook for about 25 minutes until flour is a nice brown color, shaking or stirring about twice along the way. Place ingredients 2-6 in a blender and add about 3 cups of the chicken stock. Add about 1/3 of the browned flour and liquefy the mixture. Add about half of the remaining flour, and blend until flour is assimilated (no lumps). Repeat with remaining flour. Place mixture in a sauce pan; add remaining chicken stock. Cook over low heat for about 20 minutes, or until thickened. Roux can be used in seafood or other meat gumbos, or frozen for future needs. See page 71.

<u>Notes</u>

Chapter 5

<u>Wild Edibles</u>

When it comes to "wild" food, tastes and opinions vary widely-- or maybe I should say wildly. What is one man's fancy (or woman's) is another man's poison -- both literally and figuratively. Some plant parts can make you sick as a dog if you don't know what you're doing. There are a few wild foods that are more or less unanimously selected by food gatherers when the season is right. Which ones are they?? How are they prepared?? When are they ready?? What special handling is required?? And more.... The Morel mushroom probably tops this list. Morels sell for up to $20 per pound in France; yet they grow wild in our neck of the woods. No, I don't know how many French franks that is. Come to think of it-- that's spelled francs and not like hot-dogs. Pecans may be second on the list. There are a few tricks in gathering and using wild pecans too. Wild walnuts are another food where the kernels sell for maybe $6.00 per pound. If you don't know some walnut tricks, $6.00 amounts to about fifty cents per hour in labor if you do your own. I've seen people lose 10 pounds trying to crack and eat black walnuts -- just joking of course.

In the way of herbs, there are wild garlic, wild onions, wild sage, sand plums. Whoops! Sand plums got on the wrong side of the period. Sand plums, wild blackberries -- poke greens, and more round out the list. Some plants that are found in the edible plant books may be edible, but who wants to brave chiggers and poison ivy to find them? Me, I'd rather go to the supermarket and buy some tame stuff. Take juniper berries for instance. Which other wild foods aren't worth the effort? Robins and other birds may be partial to juniper berries, and as far as I'm concerned they can eat them all. The following pages shed some light on these and other wild mysteries, and tasty morsels.

Morel Mushrooms

Many people have mycophobia- a fear of mushrooms. I was such a person until I moved to Ponca City and found out that I had purchased some land known to have the famous morel. What is a morel? Here in the Ponca City area, nothing is more secret than one's morel mushroom hunting grounds. If it is wishful thinking that the rainbow ends in a pot of gold, it is even better if it ends in a morel mushroom bed.

These tasty morsels show up in the spring after the first good rain. I usually start my morel investigative ordeal about the first day of spring. March 20 or there-about. I really start looking in earnest after the first rain of a half inch or more after spring's entry. I look along the creek where old trees have rotted; where lots of leaves have fallen. Most of all, I look where these mushrooms have shown up before. Morels are virtually unmistakable. They are safe to eat as far as I know. My wife did, however, wait a day until after I ate some to see if I became deathly or even slightly sick. Then she became brave and ate some too. Here in northern Oklahoma, the morels I've seen are a grayish-brown color or a golden color. Remember my earlier statement of gold at the end of the rainbow? Well there's the proof of the pudding! Mushroom books describe a black version, but I haven't seen any in this area. Morels are hollow and have a unique honeycomb appearance.

Pan-fried Morel Mushrooms

Pre-preparation

Wash mushrooms thoroughly in salt water. Rinse. Cut lengthwise into quarters. Refrigerate in zipper plastic bag until ready to use.

Seasoned flour

Mix 1 cup flour, ½ tsp. salt, ¼ tsp. pepper.

Ingredients

1. Prepared morel mushrooms
2. 1 cup buttermilk
3. Seasoned flour
4. Bread crumbs
5. Oil for frying

Pour oil about ½ inch deep into a skillet. Heat medium high until a bread cube sizzles. Place mushrooms and seasoned flour in a bag and shake until mushrooms are coated. Dredge mushrooms in buttermilk, then coat with bread crumbs. Place into heated oil and cook for about 2 minutes -- or until they're the shade that you like. Turn once, and cook for about 1-2 minutes until brown. Drain on paper towels and serve. Ranch or honey mustard salad dressing makes an acceptable dip if you want to contaminate the unique mushroomy flavor.

Other Morel Yummies

Use morels in other cooked mushroom recipes, such as mushroom soup, sautéed mushrooms, etc.

Other Edible Mushrooms

Earlier, I mentioned mycophobia, a fear of mushrooms. Now I'll mention another strange but related word - mycophagist. A mycophagist is a person who eats mushrooms. They know the chantrelles, the meadow mushroom, puffballs, and others. So far, I've been brave enough to eat morels. Next on my list are the puffballs. I'm not sure if I'll venture further or not; only time and bravery will tell.

Lamb's Quarters

Of all the wild greens, I think lamb's quarters are the tastiest and most unique. For best eating, pick lamb's quarters in the spring when the plants are young and tender. During the fall, the seed heads of lamb's quarters can be thrashed. The resulting small brownish-black seeds make an interesting and tasty addition to whole grain bread. A couple of tablespoons are all you need. Lamb's quarters kept lots of folks from growing hungry during the depression. The plant is weed-like and very hardy, growing shoulder high when mature-- if water is plentiful. I especially like a little green lamb's quarters in my bean soup.

Prepared Lamb's Quarters

Select tender leaves and stems, usually found near the top of the plant. Again, young plants -less than a foot high- offer the best taste. Wash thoroughly to remove any sand or dirt. Boil or steam the lamb's quarters for a minute or two. The greens are a bright deep rich green color when done. Overcooking will result in a loss of color and appeal.

Ingredients

1. 2 cups cooked lamb's quarters
2. 1 tsp. bacon fat or cooking oil
3. 2 slices of cooked bacon, crumbled (optional)
4. ¼ cup chopped onion
5. 1 Tbs. green chile
6. ½ tsp. salt
7. Pepper sauce to taste

Sauté onions in fat or oil until translucent. Add the green chile. Steam or boil the lamb's quarters for about 2 minutes, or until tender and bright green. Add cooked lamb's quarters to the onion mixture and stir until mixed. Add crumbled cooked bacon, salt, and pepper. Serves 4 unless one person eats it all. I like pepper sauce and/or vinegar as a garnish.

Poke

Poke is mysterious, or so it seems to be. Poisonous if eaten raw, poke is a tasty green if properly prepared. Some say that it has medicinal qualities. Use only young tender leaves and shoots. **Boil the leaves and pour off the water, then rinse the leaves thoroughly in cold water.** *Avoid eating other parts of the plant, including berries and roots.* I've heard that many children have used poke berries for "blood" in games and such. Cooked poke can be used in place of spinach in recipes; however, "poke salad" is possibly the most frequently used preparation method.

Ingredients for poke salad:

1. Poke greens, about 2 cups cooked, rinsed, and drained
2. 3 strips bacon
3. 1 small onion, or ½ cup green onion, chopped
4. 2 eggs, slightly beaten
5. Pepper sauce, a few shakes

Fry bacon until crisp. Reserve the grease in the pan. Drain bacon on paper towels. Sauté onion until translucent. Add poke, pepper sauce, and stir until mixed. Add eggs, crumbled bacon, and cook until eggs solidify. Season to taste with salt and pepper, and pepper sauce. Serves about 4.

Other Greens

Water cress is, in my opinion, about the only other wild green worth going after. Most other edible greens are basically survival fare. Young dandelion greens, wild lettuce, plantain, and more are certainly edible, but I think the tame stuff like leaf and head lettuce, cabbage, mustard, etc. that you get from the garden and grocery make better salads or cooked greens.

Nuts

There are several nut varieties that grow in the wild. Pecans are native to about 20 states, and can be found growing on public land in several other places. Black walnuts, hazelnuts, hickories, and a few other nut varieties can also be found growing wild in different parts of the country. Even some acorns are classed as edible by humans, but many are very bitter. I leave acorns to the squirrels. Each "native" nut tree is a variety of its own, and thus its respective nuts vary in qualities that both squirrels and humans deem desirable. Native pecans, for example, vary significantly in size, crackability, flavor, and other attributes. The same with black walnuts and others of the nut family.

Pecans

In my opinion, pecans are the *creme-de-la-creme* of the wild edible nuts. Being a pecan grower and author of a comprehensive book on pecans, could I be prejudiced? My pecan book, although directed at commercial growers and people with an interest in growing pecans, has a section entitled ***Pecans for Food.***

Fortunately, one doesn't need to have a green thumb to enjoy eating pecans. Pecans do have some calories, I'll have to admit. Fortunately again, many of the calories are derived from monounsaturated fat - the same type of fat found in olive oil. Monounsaturated fats appear to maintain or improve body levels of "good" (HDL) cholesterol and LDL/HDL ratios. Thus, I've included some pecan nutritional information just in case your spouse thinks that pecans are unhealthy. I've also included pecan buying tips -- just in case your search for the wild pecan comes up empty handed.

A human interest episode from ***Pecans - A Growers Perspective*** provides a few tips in selecting pecans for purchase, and hopefully, some other entertaining and worthwhile information. Recipes from my pecan book are included later in chapter 9. Just in case you're a pecan enthusiast, my pecan book can be ordered from: PecanQuest Publications, RR 3, Box 473, Ponca City, OK 74604. Phone: 405-767-1195.

Searching out the wild pecan

Searching out the wild pecan can be a fun experience. Native pecans are flavorful, but sometimes try a persons patience in extracting the kernels. Both wild pecans and the larger, easier to shell tame varieties are usable in the nutty delights recipes found on pages 99-107.

Pecan trees are found typically along creeks and rivers, and prefer deep lowland soil. They are most abundant in the southern and mid-southern states, and along the Mississippi drainage areas as far north as Illinois and Indiana.

Pecans usually start to ripen in October, and may be abundant one year and almost absent the next year or two. When ripe, and under normal healthy conditions, the shuck of the pecan opens up, exposing the pecan as we know it from the market. Pecans fall freely- or not so freely from their shucks. A strong wind, a tree shaker, or a flailing pole speeds up the process. If left to Nature's process, pecans may drop from the tree over an extensive period. Squirrels, crows, blue jays, and other critters usually take their share both from the tree and from the ground. Pecans that fall with the shuck attached are usually not edible. These "stick-tights" are usually insect damaged, diseased, or have been caught by an early freeze.

Storing to maintain freshness

Assuming that you've found a wild pecan bonanza, storing your catch may be a necessity. Pecans will retain their taste and color for six months or so under standard refrigeration of 35-40 degrees F. If frozen, pecans will keep for a year with little loss in quality. If stored at zero degrees Fahrenheit, pecans will stay fresh-like for two years. They may be thawed and re-frozen many times without loss in quality. Due to space, most pecans are stored as kernels. Vacuum sealing also helps to maintain freshness, and extends storage life. Nuts in the shell also maintain freshness better if they are frozen or refrigerated.

Pecans are good odor absorbers, so take care in what goes into storage with them. Avoid storage with apples, citrus, or other strong smelling fruits. If you like orange or apple flavored pecans, cohabitation in storage can accomplish your objectives.

Pecan - food value and composition

Pecans are a popular food item either eaten "straight" in their raw form or toasted. They may be even more popular as a component of other foods. A pair of kernels from one typical improved variety pecan has a calorie value of about 30. Typical in this case means 60 inshell nuts per pound with a shelling percent of 55% kernel. The wild native pecan is about half as big, with a shelling percent which averages around 40%. Calorie count for a typical wild pecan might average about 11.

Percentages of the different organic compounds and minerals vary among the different varieties, and within the same variety from year to year and place to place. The following list describes typical ranges for well filled kernels.

Composition

1. Oil is the biggest component in pecan kernels, varying from around 65% to more than 75%. Most of the oil is unsaturated (around 90% or more). The ratio of monounsaturated fat to polyunsaturated fat averages about 3:1.
2. Carbohydrate content varies from around 12% to 15%.
3. Protein, around 10%.
4. Water, 3 to 4.5%
5. Vitamins and minerals, 1 to 1.5%
6. Sodium, trace

Pecan Oil

1. Oleic acid 39 to 83%
2. Linoleic acid 10 to 49%
3. Stearic acid 1.1 to 2.9%
4. Palmitic acid 5.4 to 10.6%
5. Cholesterol, none to a trace

Oleic acid and linoleic acid together comprise about 95% of the total content of pecan oil. The percent saturated fat in pecan oil thus averages around 5%. The highest reported percent saturated fat is well below many popular vegetable oils, including corn, peanut, soybean, and cottonseed. Pecan oil compares favorably with olive oil in percent monounsaturated fat.

Cracking pecans

After gathering or purchasing whole pecans, they must be cracked to enjoy the nutritious innards. My dog can crack a pecan with her teeth, eat the kernels, and spit out the shells. She seems to find pecans out of nowhere, and does this eating bit on the living room carpet. For some reason, my wife thinks that this habit is all my fault.

Improved variety pecans (those with thin shells) can often be cracked in the hand. Native wild pecans can be attacked with pliers or a hammer, but the end result is usually smashed or pinched fingers -- and few pecan pieces big enough to eat. The art and science of cracking pecans depend on two basic variables: the pecan and the cracker. A easy to crack pecan can be difficult with the wrong technique and the wrong cracker. A hard to crack pecan can be cracked more easily with a good cracker and good technique.

The best pecan crackers apply variable pressure to both ends of an in-shell pecan simultaneously. The shell more or less implodes, leaving the kernels intact and the shell broken sufficiently to extract the kernels with no additional cracking effort. Crackers of this type can be found in many shapes and sizes. Before you buy one, test it on several different varieties.

Another satisfactory cracker from my viewpoint allows the ends on the pecan to be cut first, then the body to be lightly cracked. Although slower, a similar percentage of unblemished halves can be extracted. Another handy tool is a 'pecan-picker-outer' made by the J.C. Baker Tool Co., Victoria, Texas. It is relatively inexpensive, and a fingernail saver for sure.

I often get asked the question, "what should I look for when buying pecans in the shell?" The following episode should give you a few pointers, and hopefully a more enjoyable reading experience than looking at a factual list.

A Trip to the Pecan Store

When we're on the road, I keep a sharp eye out for towns that are known for antiques. I secretly plan a path that avoids these towns. My wife can't pass up an antique store. I figure with pecans around, there are better things to do than look at antiques. But then, I can never pass up a pecan store. My wife has figured out my game and now she plans which towns we go through. She tries to avoid towns that have pecans.

Marriage is a wonderful series of compromises. Now we occasionally find a store that has both pecans and antiques. I even swear that I've even seen antique pecans for sale. Most antique proprietors want their wares to sound even older than they really are. These pecans were advertised, "new crop". Maybe the sign was antique, although it appeared to be freshly painted.

Now don't get me wrong. Most pecan dealers that reside in pecan country have good quality pecans. They may advertise both natives and improved varieties. Orchards that have retail outlets are probably the most accurate when it comes to having properly labeled varieties.

In bad years, retail orchard outlets will sell imported pecans. By imported, I mean that they were brought from other nearby orchards or other areas of the country. I've seen few cases where imported pecans were intentionally passed off as being locally grown. In many instances, the pecans won't be labeled at all. If asked, the proprietor will usually tell you the truth.

There are a few stores that may try to take advantage of the buyer's naivety. Sometimes the sign outside will read "PECANS-FRESH LOCAL CROP". Inside will be several bins of nuts of which one bin may be filled with fresh local nuts. Other bins may have nuts grown two or three years ago that have been in cold storage. I guess they were fresh then and local to some place. An educated consumer will soon to learn to recognize misleading advertising and will be able to assess fair price for fair value.

Now for my story. We were traveling down a state road west of Houston, Texas. It was the first week in November. Prime pecan time! Trying hard, I couldn't keep the car from turning into a roadside market that read, "FRESH LOCAL

PECANS". Better yet, the next building adjacent to the market said, "ANTIQUES".

My wife headed for the antique store. Guess where I went? I could hear the clackety-clack of pecan crackers going in earnest. Nothing quite sounds like pecan crackers. Some would say, "thank goodness". As I entered the doors, a gentle breeze caused by overhead fans and a few box fans was a welcome relief. Southern Texas can be warm even in November, at least compared with northern Oklahoma.

Once I was inside, the unique smell of an open air market was apparent. The blended smells of fresh vegetables that were still in season were like perfume. A pile of leftover pumpkins stood in one corner, some starting to show their age a little bit. Against one wall were the bins of pecans. I saw labels that said: DESIRABLE, WICHITA, WESTERN, SIOUX, CHEYENNE, SUCCESS, KIOWA, and CHOCTAW (all improved pecan varieties, or "papershell pecans" - as they're sometimes called). Out in the open area stood a display that said "LOCAL NATIVES". I was told that Pawnee had come and gone when I asked about them. Pawnee ripens very early in this part of the country.

Most of the varieties were labeled properly, but there were a few exceptions. Desirables (a pecan variety) were really Choctaws (another pecan variety). The Choctaws looked a little like Kiowa nuts from another area. Success nuts looked a little like Barton, but I was only sure that they weren't of the Success variety. I picked up about a half pound each variety and carried them to the counter. The Desirable Choctaws were the most expensive at $2.89 per pound. After I got the nuts back to the car, I cracked open a few of each variety. The Desirable Choctaws were the worst of the lot in quality. They were either old or had spent too much time on the ground before harvest. Kernel color was rather dark and somewhat mottled. As usual, Cheyenne and Sioux looked the best and tasted the best. They were $2.39 per pound. Of course well cared for Choctaw and Desirable pecans are usually top quality also.

My wife was still seeking out antiques so I went back to the market to nose around some more. The onions looked as good as they always do in this part of the country, so I put a sack of

41

onions in my basket. "Look at that", I thought, "fresh okra at this time of the year. Wonder if it will keep all the way back to Oklahoma?" My basket received a bag of okra.

A man who seemed a little foreign to this neck of the woods was still at the pecan display when I came by again. This time he had about ten pounds of the Desirable Choctaws sacked up. I was about to decide whether to stick my nose where it didn't belong when the man made a comment. "I'm just going to have to ask you why you bought all those sacks with a few pecans in each one." I told him I was a pecan grower in Oklahoma and wanted to see how quality varied for different cultivars (varieties) in this part of the country. "Did you say cul-te-barrs. What in the world is that?" I didn't know my OKIE accent was that bad. I changed my tune from cultivars to "kinds", and added a little further information. I threw in the word "varieties" just for good measure.

The man said, " I heard these Desirables are the best. Must be, since they're the most expensive. By the way, if you're a grower why are you buying these pecans anyway?" Good question. I guess it's the same reason that a lady with 24 cats buys another one. She wants to see how it compares. I ignored his question and added a comment. You know, out of all those pecans, I thought those over there were the best (pointing to the CHEYENNE and SIOUX signs). He replied, "those little ole things". I answered back, "they're smaller, but they shell out easy, taste good, look pretty -- and they're cheaper."

He wasn't looking too impressed. I said, " My wife's still at that shop over there. Come on out to my car and I'll show you a few comparisons." He said, "My wife is over there too." We both trusted each other I guess since we had that one similarity. Wives that like antiques.

I showed him samples of the three varieties, and let him take the taste test. He said with a mouth full of pecans, "Y'know, these little fellers do taste purty ---- good." The Desirable Choctaws that I cracked were about like the original sample; a little off color and a little stale in taste.

He was munching on a few of them when my wife arrived with a little brown bag with some sort of glassware. At least it was a *little* brown bag. I bid the man good-bye as he was swallowing the last morsel. His wife still hadn't come out yet.

As we drove away, I saw the man dumping out his sack full of Desirable Choctaws, and started filling it with Cheyennes and Siouxs. At least he saved a little money for the next antique store.

This story has a few morals. First, don't buy a bunch of in-shell pecans without cracking open two or three to inspect quality. Second, all pecans may not be labeled correctly. Take my book along and check them out. The third moral says that the most expensive pecans aren't always the best. I'll only tell you that the fourth moral has to do with antiques.

Black Walnut Baseball

Black walnut trees exist over a broad area of the USA. Officially known as the Eastern black walnut, some may know its nuts from black walnut ice cream, or from skinny squirrels. I'm not sure how a squirrel makes a living eating something as hard to crack and shell out as a typical wild black walnut. Most squirrels are smart enough to know that my improved variety black walnuts are far easier fare than the wild ones. Even the dumbest of squirrels eat all the pecans first.

Back in Arkansas where my mom grew up, we used black walnuts as baseballs. Most of the time, we could use a single walnut over and over without it breaking. Sure put a lot of dents in the bat though. I can remember this one wild walnut tree that I found. Its nuts were pretty good sized - about 20 per pound after the husk was removed. It was also almost round-- a perfect baseball. I brought a bucketful to my grandma's house, then knocked the husks off with the help of my shoes and the gravel driveway. I ended up with brown stain on my hands as usual. Walnut stain outlasted lye soap, and everything else that mom tried to use before we went to church on Sunday. Walnut stain is indelible to say the least, so it's best to use rubber gloves when dehusking walnuts.

Those particular walnuts made lousy baseballs. They cracked when hit with a bat by my eight year old cousin -- and she was a girl! It cost my uncle a whole pack of ice cream bars to find out where that tree was. I might mention that even when cracked with a baseball bat, the kernels usually came out in quarters.

Thus the moral to this story is to look for that exceptional black walnut tree, and to have a tough baseball bat. In reality, if you are a seeker of wild black walnuts, the first thing on your shopping list should be a reputable black walnut cracker. If a skinny squirrel could operate one of the two different versions that I've used, it would probably need to increase the level of aerobic exercise in a hurry -- that is if a sleek squirrelish figure is to be maintained. Such a durable and ingenious piece of equipment costs about $50 (1995 prices). This sum of money can probably be saved quickly in doctor bills. It's amazing how big a knot a flying black walnut can raise when improperly smacked with a hammer. Replacing the neighbors' windows can also be expensive.

If you aren't lucky enough to find the exceptional black walnut tree in your territory, you can make one in a few years by grafting a reasonably sized walnut tree with improved black walnut scions. A scion is a cutting from a known black walnut variety. Since this is a cookbook, you'll have to learn grafting from my pecan book or someplace else. Grafting is easy and fun to do. Emma Kay, Elmer Myers, Rowher, Ogden, and Sparrow are just a few of many varieties that you can choose from. Thomas is probably the most famous of the black walnut varieties, but in my opinion, is inferior to the others that I mentioned.

Tricks of the black walnut trade

These are not old wives' or crazy husbands' tales! The following facts are helpful when harvesting and preparing black walnuts:

1. Black walnuts are ripe when the husk starts to soften. When the husk dents with pressure from your thumb, the walnut is ready to harvest. Walnuts will usually fall to the ground shortly after they are ripe.

2. Remove the husk promptly. Walnuts are messy and hard to clean, but the job is easier if done promptly. The walnut kernels also retain a lighter color if the husk is removed promptly.

3. Drop the freshly husked walnuts in a bucket of water. If they float, they probably have little or no kernel. Use the floaters as baseballs or chunking missiles.

4. Let the walnuts dry in a well ventilated place for a couple of weeks. If they stay in a heated house all winter, the kernels may shatter when the nuts are cracked. Store the cleaned nuts in a cool place.

5. If you don't get around to husking and cleaning your walnuts promptly, they are still usable -- but more work. Kernels may also be darker than they would have been otherwise. Knock the husks off with your shoed feet. Maybe the word should be shod, but I remembered the phrase, "the horses were shod." Shoed, shod, whatever. You then finish cleaning the nuts with a wire brush. I wear leather gloves to minimize wire brushed fingers. If you want the nuts really clean, soak the partially cleaned nuts in water for an hour or so, then use the wire brush again. **The float test doesn't work on walnuts that have dried out;** however, the best nuts will float lower in the water. Some very well filled nuts may even sink.

6. Use a cracker designed for walnuts. Eat and enjoy; you earned every morsel.

Some recipes in this book call for black walnuts; for example, the choco-nutaholic cookies and pinanna nut muffins. Black walnuts are typically stronger in flavor than pecans, so fewer are needed to flavor a recipe. Use them in homemade ice-cream, or they can be substituted for pecans in whole or in part for pecan pie. If there's a squirrel that you dislike, leave it your hardest and most difficult walnuts. Squirrels are masters at detecting empty walnuts, so you can't trick them with the floaters.

Black Walnuts -- messy to clean

Good walnuts don't float

Trick your favorite squirrel

Remove the husk promptly

Walnut baseball anyone??

Use a good cracker

Asparagus

One of spring's blessings is fresh asparagus. Whether from the wild, from the garden, or from the grocery, asparagus is a unique vegetable. I've seen it growing wild here in Oklahoma in several different environments. When we bought our land in Osage County, asparagus was growing wild in a couple of places. Since asparagus is a perennial plant, it can be found in the same place year after year. Stalks can be picked until about the first of June. After that, stalks should be left to mature so that they can nourish the plants for the next season. I've seen edible stalks as early as the first of April. One way to predict when to start looking in the wild is to plant some of the tame stuff in your yard. When the tame plants begin production, start looking for asparagus in the wild. Wild plants may start to show a few days later than those grown in the garden due to additional cover (dead weeds and grass) that delays ground warmth in unmanaged territory, and sometimes in my garden. Pick the stalks by cutting close to or below ground level. Stalks should be no more than a foot tall (preferably 6-8 inches), with a tight tip. When left to mature, the stalks become fern like. Asparagus grows like sixty when the weather reaches 90 or more degrees. I've even seen it grow before my eyes. Ha, you say? Well it's true! Later, small berries are produced that turn from green to deep orange.

Preparation

Wash the stalks in salted water to remove any sand or other grit. My favorite preparation method is simple and delicious. Boil or steam the stalks for a few minutes until crisp-tender. Serve with butter or your favorite butter substitute.

Other recipes include serving with hollandaise sauce, cream sauce, etc. Cream of asparagus soup is also worth the time to prepare it. Most cream of asparagus soup recipes that I've tried result in about the same end product.

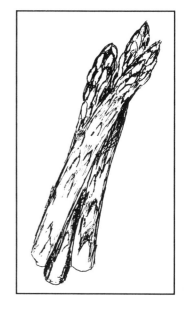

Wild Seasonings

Based on historical readings, early man discovered the value of various wild herbs and other wild plants. Native Americans gathered herbs for both nutrition and for healing. Many tame herbs are selected specimens of their wild predecessors. I've spotted wild garlic in many areas. In fact, it grows almost weedlike on my Osage County land. Wild onion is also common in our area. Some onion and garlic look-alikes are poisonous, so collect only those plants that have a distinctive onion or garlic odor. Use the wild versions in recipes that call for the tame stuff. Wild onions can be used in place of scallions or green onions. Wild garlic typically has small cloves, so it's best to first rub the cloves off of the main stalk, and mince in a food processor or press with a garlic press.

I've seen basil and sage growing wild, but the plants may have spread to the wild from cultivated gardens. There's lots of sage brush in the western states, but this plant is different than the sage we see at Thanksgiving.

I find that a small herb garden is much handier than hunting for the wild versions. However, if wild versions are abundant nearby, it's probably worth the trouble to pick and dehydrate specimens that aren't used immediately. Rub the dried specimens through a colander and place the herbal results in bottles or plastic zipper bags. Save the stems, etc. for your smoker.

Oklahoma countryside

herb garden

Sand Plums and Other Wild Plums

Back in Amarillo, we called the low growing plum thickets wild plums. Here in Oklahoma, almost everybody calls them sand plums. Since the larger growing American plum also grows here, I guess the different nomenclature distinguishes one from the other. Sand plum jelly, in my opinion, is unsurpassed. Nothing in the jelly world looks prettier or tastes better. Fruits here in Oklahoma usually mature mid to late summer.

Pick fruits when they start to turn reddish in color. A mixture of ripe (somewhat soft) and firm plums is best for jelly. Plums have a good flavor when ripe, but there's usually more seed than fruit. Plum curculios (small weevils) often lay eggs inside the fruit, which in turn develop into small disgusting white worm-like critters. Beware of both the worms and wasps. Wasps prefer plum thickets to many other places. They get mad as hornets when you invade their domain. Wasps and hornets amount to about the same thing when it comes to inflicting pain.

Plum thickets are easy to spot in the spring, when they are profusely covered with clusters of small white flowers. Remember where you saw them, then start to look again around the Fourth of July for plums. Early freezes sometimes zap all the blossoms before the plums set.

Plum Jelly

Wash, then boil the plums with about a cup of water per quart of plums. The presence of curculio worms (larvae) matter to some and not to others. The more robust individuals say that after all, the little critters have eaten plums all their lives. Boiling also sterilizes them good and proper. The finicky plum pickers pick out the wormy fruit before proceeding. Now you can wonder - did they or didn't they - when you get a gift of that special jar of plum jelly.

Cook the plums and water for about 20 minutes. Smush the plums, and place the smushed results in a jelly bag. Extract the juice, and prepare jelly according to your favorite pectin instructions. Note: My jelly will usually set without the addition of pectin. I use 1 tsp. lemon and 1 cup of sugar per cup of juice.

48

Blackberries

Blackberries also top the list when it comes to wild edibles. My, but they're tasty. I often wonder, why do the biggest and best blackberries always exist in the hardest to reach parts of the thicket? Luckily, I have some wild blackberry thickets on my land. I can run the bush-hog through the thicket from time to time to clear access paths. This opens up the brambles for easier picking. Wild blackberries grow on about the thorniest plants alive. Needless to say, wear heavy long sleeved shirts and tough trousers when in the berry patch.

Several varieties of berries exist in our neck of the woods. Some ripen in early summer, and others ripen later-- clear up till mid-August. Some berries are produced on low growing vines, or canes, as they're called. Others grow on upright canes that reach head-high or taller. The only drawback, once they're in the basket, is the seeds. Blackberries do have fair sized seeds. Seeds can be "filtered" out with an appropriate sieve, strainer, or colander.

Use blackberries to make jams, jellies, cobblers, or eat straight off the bush. Add a little ice cream to the cobbler, or to a big bowl of fresh blackberries.

Blackberry jelly

Boil the berries. Add little or no water. Smash or blenderize the cooked berries. Strain the berries through cheese cloth or a jelly bag and collect the juice. Pectin is required to ensure a good gel. Use the recipe on your favorite pectin package. I use about 1¼ cups of sugar per cup of juice.

Blackberry jam

Blackberry jam makes more efficient use of those hard earned berries that you scratched your hands and arms picking. I have a dislike for jelly with lots of seeds, so I sieve my berries after they're cooked. Again, pectin is required for a sure jell. Process according to the pectin directions. I use the same sugar/pulp ratio as for blackberry jelly.

Blackberry Cobbler

I like pie crust as a topping for cobbler. Use the recipe for crust on page 103. You can also use a biscuit type crust from your favorite recipes, or other adaptations.

Ingredients

1. 4 cups of blackberries, or blackberry pulp.
2. 1 cup of sugar (see below for a low sugar version)
3. ¼ tsp. salt
4. 1 tsp. cinnamon (optional)
5. 1½ Tbs. cornstarch (use less for a juicier cobbler)
6. 1 Tbs. butter/margarine
7. Pie crust or other topping

Cook blackberries over low heat for about 5 minutes, or until berries become juicy. Mix sugar and cornstarch. Add mixture to berries, and cook for a few minutes until mixture bubbles. Add butter, and stir until butter melts. Pour into a 9*9 baking pan. Roll out pie crust and cut into strips or other workable pieces. Cover berry mixture, using whatever creative design appeals to you. I like a patchwork pattern. Sprinkle a little sugar and cinnamon over the crust surface. Bake at 400° F for about 35-40 minutes, or until the crust is brown and the blackberries bubble.

Low sugar version

Use 1-2 Tbs. sugar with the cornstarch, and prepare as above. After the cobbler comes out of the oven, sprinkle on your favorite sugar substitute.

Persimmons

Some people like persimmons; others don't. Most possums (spelled opossums) and raccoons that I know, and even some that I don't know, love persimmons. I was smart and grafted improved variety American persimmons onto my wild versions. Weber, Garretson, Yates, Wabash, and Early Golden are some of the varieties that I chose. The fruits on improved varieties are bigger and have fewer seeds than the native varieties. I tried some of the big, huge Japanese varieties too, but most froze out.

I was dumb to think that the possums and raccoons wouldn't go after my super-persimmons. Turns out, these critters are good judges of persimmon flesh. They eat the improved stuff, and leave the little ole natives for me. Hopefully, I've now grafted enough for all of us. What does one do with a persimmon? One does not eat an American persimmon before it turns soft and has wrinkled skin. It's usually best to wait until they've been nipped by a FROST. A green persimmon will pucker up your mouth for a good while. The improved varieties are very tasty when picked or picked-up at the right time. Some wild natives are also better than others, so look for the best trees and remember their location.

Persimmon trees have unique bark that looks like a montage of squarish blocks. Once you know what one persimmon tree looks like, others are easy to spot.

Persimmon Pudding

Pick 2 quarts of wild or improved variety persimmons. You will need more small seedy persimmons than the fleshier ones. Remove the calyx (cap) from each one. Wash the persimmons carefully, especially if you've picked grounded specimens. Run the persimmons through a colander to separate pulp from seeds and skins. Hopefully, you'll extract 2 cups or more of pulp. Add 1 tsp. lemon concentrate or lemon juice and blend well.

Ingredients

1. 1 egg
2. ½ cup sugar
3. ½ tsp. vanilla
4. 3 Tbs. melted butter/margarine
5. 2 cups of persimmon pulp/with lemon juice
6. 1 cup milk
7. 1½ cups flour
8. ½ tsp. salt
9. 1 tsp. cinnamon
10. Sprinkle of cloves (optional)
11. 1½ tsp. baking powder

Beat egg, gradually adding sugar, until the mixture is fluffy - about 3-5 minutes. Add vanilla, persimmon pulp, and milk. Beat slowly until well blended. Add flour, baking powder, salt, and spices. Add melted butter and beat for about two minutes. Pour into a 9*9 baking dish that has been coated with cooking spray. Bake at 350°F for about 45 minutes, or until a knife comes out clean. Serve with cream or whipped topping. If you don't like persimmons, substitute pumpkin for a tasty dessert.

Other Persimmon Options

Persimmon pulp can be substituted for the bananas in the pineanna nutty recipe (page 101) for an interesting variation. Use persimmon pulp in place of pumpkin or part of the pumpkin in recipes. Freeze the pulp/ lemon juice for future use.

Elderberries

Many people have heard of elderberry wine. I've heard of it but have never seen or tasted any. Many sources say that elderberry wine is super. To be truthful, I'm not a very big fan of Oklahoma elderberries. American elderberries are the type that grow here. There is also a blue elderberry; maybe they taste better. American elderberries grow like weeds on my land. They are a pretty, shrub-like plant with attractive foliage and large white flowers. Elderberries start to blossom about the first of June in Oklahoma. The blossoms offer an interesting dessert dish or snack. I like the blossoms much better than the fruit. Beware of bees when gathering elderberry blossoms.

American elderberry fruit ripens to a deep purple-black color in late summer. Borne in massive clusters, the small berries can be picked in a hurry. As I said earlier, the raw berries aren't my favorite. They're supposed to be better dried or cooked. The juice is a pretty color, and can be made into jelly. Add 2 parts apple juice to one part elderberry juice.

Fritter Fried Elderberry Blossoms

Harvest blossom clusters when in full bloom. Place in a large plastic bag out of the sun. Blossoms wilt quickly in the summer heat. Wash blossoms; then shake and pat dry with paper towels.

Ingredients

1. 8-10 elderberry blossom clusters with stem intact
2. Flour for dusting
3. 1 egg
4. 1 Tbs. vegetable oil
5. 1 cup flour
6. ½ tsp. salt
7. 1 tsp. baking powder
8. 1¼ cups milk
9. 1 Tbs. sugar

Mix items 3-9 to form a thin fritter batter. Pour into a shallow dish. Dust blossom clusters with flour. Hold clusters by their stems, and dip into the fritter batter. Shake off excess batter. Fry in a deep pan or fryer at 375° until lightly browned. Sprinkle with powdered sugar and serve.

Chokecherries and Black Cherries

These two wild cherry varieties are a far cry from their tame counterparts when it comes to edibility right off the tree. Both chokecherry and black cherry fruit are borne in a cluster-like arrangement as illustrated in the sketch below. The chokecherry is fairly common over much of the USA, while the black cherry grows mainly in the USA's eastern half.

Black cherries are typically almost black when ripe and a quarter inch in diameter. They can grow bigger in a wet year. They are juicy, but slightly bitter. A little sugar or sweetener makes eating them more tolerable. Pits are egg-shaped, and occupy a large part of the fruit's volume. In other words, be prepared to pick lots of cherries for a little edible flesh. Pitting four cups of black cherries for a pie could turn into a career.

If black cherries border between edible and inedible, chokecherries hover even closer to the inedible side. The little bit of flesh that clings to the egg-shaped pit is very astringent. Maybe that's why they're called chokecherries. They too are almost black when ripe.

Cherry Jelly

Now, chokecherry and black cherry jelly is another thing -- a shining light in the jelly world. First, add about a cup of water to a quart of unpitted (thank goodness) cherries. Boil the combination for about 30 minutes, smushing cherries along the way. Strain through a jelly bag. Is this little dab of cherry juice enough? Wait and read the next line. Use equal parts apple juice and black cherry juice. Use one part choke cherry juice to two parts apple juice. Apples fill a bucket much more quickly than wild cherries. Follow the directions included with your pectin box. Use about 1¼ cups sugar to 1 cup of juice. The jelly is, sure enough, a worthwhile reward for all that effort.

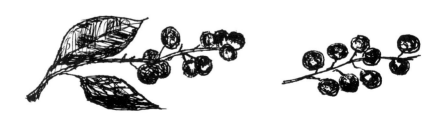

Chapter 6

<u>Traditional Favorites</u>

Some recipes come and go, but a few have been around since man decided that cooked food is more appealing than raw buffalo. Chicken and noodles or dumplings have been popular since chickens and flour were invented. A bowl of chicken and... (noodles or dumplings) seems always to disappear completely when served. I personally never seem to tire of this basic recipe.

Fried chicken also falls into this category. I remember it in older days as a traditional Sunday dinner. Mom always hated converting live chicken into a product for the table, so dad usually did it for her. Talk about fresh chicken! We didn't need to wonder if 20 degree storage constituted fresh or frozen nomenclature. A key secret is to marinate the chicken for a few hours prior to frying it. Marinade helps to maintain a juicy product, and enhances the flavor. An added touch is to dip the marinated chicken in buttermilk for a crispier product, prior to the frying process.

Chili has also been around the Southwest since the trail drive days, and maybe even earlier. I've heard that the spices and red chile also acted as both a tenderizer and a preservative for the not-so-tender trail drive beef. The following herbal chili recipe is somewhat unique and is one of the best that I've ever seen -- and tasted, come to think of it.

Then there's Steak Diane. Add a good spinach salad to this selection, and you're in tall cotton -- or maybe even Utopia. Pot roast, chicken fried steak, meat loaf, and more round out the list, but so far I've never concocted a unique enough recipe to outdo other recipe sources.

> "Some recipes have been around since man decided that cooked food is more appealing than raw buffalo."

Chicken and Dumplings or Noodles

Ingredients

1. 1 Tbs. cooking oil
2. One small onion, food processorized with shredding blade.
3. One carrot, likewise processed
4. One stalk of celery, ditto
5. 1 Tbs. fresh cilantro or parsley, chopped
6. 2 cloves garlic, minced
7. 1½ tsp. *Rice's Chicken Enhancer™*
8. 6-8 cups of chicken stock
9. One smallish potato, blender liquefied in two cups of stock
10. 1-2 cups chopped boiled chicken
11. Noodles and/or dumplings

Noodles/dumplings

I use frozen noodles, or dumplings made according to recipes on a baking mix box. My wife likes the packaged noodles/dumplings found in the pasta section at the grocery store. We usually split up the stock and other ingredients and each use our favorite "noodlings".

Putting it together

Cook celery, onion, and carrots in the oil for about 3 minutes. Add remaining ingredients, except chicken, and cook for about 45 minutes, using a good pot with lid. Add chicken and noodles or dumplings and cook for about 12-20 minutes; or until noodles/dumplings are done. Follow recipe directions for dumplings; recipes usually say to cook uncovered for about 10 minutes - then cook covered for about ten minutes. Enough for 4, with second helpings.

Fried Chicken

A basic requirement for superb fried chicken is a top quality, properly prepared chicken. If you're a fan of white meat, then choose the breast pieces, and/or wings. Learning to cut up a whole fryer is worth the experience - training, or whatever. If this skill is beyond you, choose a cutup specimen. Fresh chickens usually work better than the frozen kind. Soak your chicken in salted ice water for at least an hour, or put your chicken, covered in salted water, in the fridge. This salt water step is vitally important. Rinse the chicken in cold water, pat dry, and then place your chicken in marinade (see page 115). It's best to let the chicken stand in the marinade for an hour or so, turning once. **For a crispier product, dip the marinated chicken in buttermilk.**

Dusting Ingredients

1. 1 cup flour
2. 1 tsp. *Rice's Chicken Enhancer™*
3. 1 tsp. salt
4. ½ tsp. pepper

Mix the above ingredients and place in a plastic bag. Add the marinated chicken, two or three pieces at a time, and shake until the chicken is coated.

The Cooker and Cooking

Choose a proper skillet. I like the modern ones, such as TFAL®. Cook a couple of strips of bacon (optional) and retain the grease in the cooker. Add about a half inch of veggie oil and heat to about 375 degrees (medium high). Add chicken skin side down. Reduce heat to about 325 degrees (medium) and cook covered, for about 10 minutes. Uncover, increase the heat to about 375 again, and cook for about 5-6 minutes. Turn the pieces and cook uncovered until brown (8-10 minutes). Turn the pieces if necessary for uniformity in browning. Make cream gravy from about 2 Tbs. of the drippings, ¼ cup of the seasoned flour, and 2-3 cups of milk.

Spinach Salad

One of my favorites! A secret is in the onions. Mild, meaty Texas 1015, or sweet purple onions make a difference.

Salad Ingredients

1. One bunch (about a pound) of de-stemmed spinach
2. A few sprigs of cilantro, chopped (optional)
3. 8 oz. can Mandarin oranges, drained
4. ½ onion, chopped or sliced thin
5. ¼ cup sliced almonds or chopped pecans, toasted (275° -15 min.)
6. ½ cup sliced mushrooms

Dressing Ingredients

1. 2 slices bacon
2. 3 Tbs. vegetable oil
3. ½ cup cider or wine vinegar
4. 2 Tbs. raspberry vinegar (or other vinegar)
5. ½ tsp. corn starch
6. ½ onion, chopped
7. ¼ tsp. salt
8. ¼-½ cup sugar, depending on your taste (a sugar free sweetener can be substituted if added just after cooking)

Dressing preparation

Fry bacon until crisp; remove and drain on paper towel. Retain the grease. Over low heat, add oil, and sauté onions until translucent. Add corn starch. Stir until cornstarch is absorbed. Add vinegars, stir, and heat until boiling. Add sugar (or sweetener), and salt. Remove from heat. Stir until sugar dissolves.

Salad preparation

Wash and drain spinach thoroughly. Add chopped onions, cilantro, toasted nuts, Mandarin oranges, mushrooms, crumbled bacon. Toss thoroughly. Warm dressing almost to boiling and pour over salad mix. Serves 2-4.

Herbal Steak Diane

Ingredients

1. Round steak or sirloin steak (1-1½ pounds)
2. 1 Tbs. vegetable oil
3. 1 Tbs. dry mustard
4. 1-2 tsp. *Rice's Beef Enhancer ™*
5. 1 tsp. black pepper
6. 1 Tbs. vegetable oil, if needed
7. Salt to taste
8. ½ cup sherry or other wine
9. 1 clove garlic, minced
10. 1 Tbs. Worcestershire sauce
11. 1 Tbs. lemon juice
12. ½ tsp. cornstarch
13. ½ cup water

Cut meat in serving sized pieces. Using a meat mallet, pound meat until it is about ¼ inch thick. Sprinkle both sides of meat liberally with mustard, beef enhancer, and black pepper. The mustard and other flavors are absorbed better if they are beaten into the steak, but cleanup is harder. Heat skillet to medium high until a drop of water sizzles. Add oil and heat for a minute. Cook steak pieces one or two at a time until well browned on both sides. Add second batch of oil if necessary along the way. Add browned steak pieces and remaining ingredients. Simmer for a few minutes. Remove steak. Shake cornstarch and water together in a closed container until any lumps disappear. Add cornstarch mixture to skillet and heat until thickened, stirring often. Serve resulting sauce separately, or pour over the meat. Serves about 4.

White Herbal Chili

This recipe is a tasty alternative to the more conventional red chili.

Ingredients

1. 1 Tbs. vegetable oil
2. 2 cloves garlic
3. 1 large onion, quartered
4. 1 stalk celery, cut into 4-5 pieces
5. ¼ cup green chiles, chopped (less for a milder chili)
6. 2 Tbs. *Rice's Green Chile Blend™*
7. 1 Tbs. *Rice's Chicken Enhancer™*
8. 1 tsp. *Rice's Molé Blend™*
9. 8 cups chicken stock
10. 1 cup dry navy beans
11. 1 Boned chicken, chopped - about 2 cups
12. 1 tsp. salt
13. water
14. 1 cup sour cream (optional)

Using the metal blade of a food processor, mince garlic. Add onion, celery, and chop until about pea size. Heat oil in a large sauce pan, and sauté chopped mixture until onion becomes translucent. Add ingredients 5-9. Add beans, removing any bad ones beforehand. Cook until beans are soft- about 2-3 hours. Add chicken, salt, and enough water to reach the consistency that you like. Cook over low heat for about 30 minutes, or until mixture bubbles. Stir in sour cream and serve. Makes about 8 regular or 4 king-size servings.

If this recipe is too hot for your taste buds, add less green chile blend.

Herbal Chili

Ingredients

1. 5 Tbs. *Rice's Red Herbal Chile Blend™*
2. 2 pounds ground beef and/or prepared beef chuck (see below) -A mix of shredded and ground beef works best.
3. 1 medium onion (about 3/4 cup), chopped
4. 2-3 cloves garlic, minced
5. 1 stalk celery, minced finely
6. 2 Tbs. green chile, chopped
7. 1 can (16 oz.) tomatoes or 3 cups peeled fresh tomatoes
8. 2 cups chicken stock or broth
9. 2 cups water
10. 2 chicken bouillon cubes
11. 2 Tbs. raspberry vinegar, or red wine vinegar
12. ½ cup red wine

Using a large pot, brown the ground beef. Add prepared chuck. Sauté onions, garlic, and celery in the grease left after browning the meat. Cook until onion turns translucent. Stir in all the remaining ingredients. Simmer over low heat for at least two hours. Serves about 4 - 6 people.

Prepared chuck

Remove ground beef and brown cubes of chuck or other beef. Cool and shred beef cubes with the metal blade of a food processor. Shredded beef provides a texture that I like.

Variations

1. Liquefy water, onion, celery, garlic, and green chile in a blender. Add directly to the beef without sautéing.
2. Substitute ground and shredded turkey for the beef.
3. Substitute apple juice for the water.
4. Add 1-2 cups cooked pinto or other beans.

Freezing instructions

This recipe freezes well. I usually make a big batch and freeze several servings for future use. Use zipper plastic bags or foil containers. I find it best to freeze without the beans.

Bob's Pancakes

Perhaps the best pancakes that I've ever eaten were in the home of our good friends, Bob and Jane Hayman. Maybe part of the wonder was due to the Fort Collins, Colorado setting. Fort Collins has always been one of my favorite places. I could have said that these breakfast wonders were cooked on the banks of the Laramie River, but of course I'd be lying. Food always tastes better along the banks of a perfect trout stream. I'm not sure that my re-creation of these pancakes at 1000 feet in Oklahoma is as good as the results at almost a mile high in Colorado, but they're still the best ever. Ask my grandson, who would rather eat these pancakes than go to McDonalds® -- and I didn't even include a prize!! By the way, I gave my grandson the plain old round version, rather than a pancake shaped like a dinosaur.

These instructions are in Bob's own words. Hopefully, his pancake talent will be absorbed into this page -- then into your own results.

Dry Ingredients

1. 1 cup all purpose flour
2. 1 Tbs. sugar
3. 1¼ tsp. baking soda
4. ¼ tsp. salt, or to taste

Note: for altitudes at Fort Collins (approximately 5000 ft.) and higher, reduce the baking soda to 1 teaspoon. For super-high altitudes, i.e. Alma, Colorado (approximately 10,000 ft.), your guess is as good as mine.

Wet Ingredients

1. 2 eggs
2. 1½ cups buttermilk
3. 1 Tbs. vegetable oil

Mix the dry stuff and the wet stuff separately and thoroughly. Gently stir the dry stuff into the wet stuff. Stop just before all the lumps disappear. Bake on medium-high heat. Garnish with soft butter and warm syrup. OhBoy!

Chapter 7

Soups

When winter arrives on the scene, nothing to me tastes better than a good bowl of soup. Often in summer, nothing to me tastes better than a good bowl of soup -- fresh tomato soup for instance. One of my favorite soups is the Chinese favorite, egg drop. I've eaten both good and bad versions. One of the best that I've eaten is right here in Ponca City at the Hunan Garden and Hunan Restaurants. Their versions contain vegetables -- just the right amount of peas, green beans, carrots, corn, etc., in a good stock. I've tried to make egg drop soup myself a few times, but the results don't compare with what I can purchase. Needless to say, I hardly ever make egg drop soup. Otherwise, good soups are hard to find in most restaurants that I visit. So I make my own.

Soups listed in this book for the most part make complete, well balanced meals. My favorite is the tortilla soup listed as the first recipe in this section. It has nine vegetables included, plus herbs and garlic--certainly a meal in itself. The other soups are also tasty and nutritious, each with its own purpose and flavor.

Tortilla Soup

The stock

1. 2 medium onions, chopped
2. 1 stalk celery, chopped
3. 3 cloves garlic, minced finely
4. 1 Tbs. olive oil
5. 4 cups chicken stock
6. 4 beef bouillon cubes
7. 1 tsp. salt
8. 2 cups crushed tomatoes, fresh or canned
9. 1/4 cup green chiles, chopped
10. 1 Tbs. *Rice's Red Herbal Chile Blend™*
11. 1/4 cup chopped fresh cilantro

A food processor is handy for mincing garlic and chopping the onions and celery. Start the chopping blade and drop the garlic through the chute. After the garlic is minced, add the celery and onion and chop to a medium texture. Sauté onions, garlic, and celery mix in olive oil over medium heat until the onions become translucent. (about 3-4 minutes). Add remaining ingredients except for the cilantro, and cook over low heat for about 30 minutes -- or longer if time permits. If you want a smooth stock, puree in a blender or food processor until it reaches a consistency that you like. One of the blenders that works in a pan is handy for this. For a chunky stock, leave as is. Add the cilantro, and re-heat. I usually make a double or triple batch of the stock and freeze for later use.

Continued-next page

Tortilla Soup- continued

The vegetables and chicken

1. One medium potato, boiled, baked or microwaved
2. 1 zucchini, cut into thin narrow strips
3. 1 yellow squash, ditto
4. 2 carrots shredded
5. 10-12 spinach leaves, cut in strips
6. Vegetable oil spray
7. 1 cup diced cooked chicken

Cool the potato, and cut into bite-size pieces. Brown the potato pieces in a pan sprayed with vegetable oil spray. This process keeps the potatoes from crumbling excessively. Cook the carrots in the stock for about 3 minutes. Cut the zucchini and squash into manageable lengths. Add zucchini, squash, and chicken and cook for about a minute. Place the spinach strips in the serving bowls.

Finishing up

1. 8 oz. shredded Monterey Jack or Mozzarella cheese
2. 4 corn tortillas, cut in quarter-inch strips

Fry tortilla strips a few at a time in hot vegetable oil until crisp. Do not overcook. Strips should remain a yellow color. Place shredded cheese into serving bowls along with a few tortilla strips. Pour hot stock into serving bowls. Add a few tortilla strips to the bowls and serve.

The recipe is sufficient for about 8 large bowls of soup. Since the recipe is time consuming, I usually start with prepared stock that has been frozen. We usually freeze the stock in quart size zipper plastic bags.

Beefy Vegetable Soup

The puree

1. 2 cups tomatoes
2. One pared potato, cut into pieces
3. 1 stalk celery
4. 1 cup eggplant (optional)
5. ¼ cup sweet peppers roasted, peeled, and seeded
6. One onion, chopped
7. 1 cup water

Puree all ingredients in a blender or food processor; set aside.

The vegetables

1. 1-2 potatoes cut into cubes
2. 2 carrots cut into cubes
3. 1 small can of corn -- about a cup
4. 4 or 5 okra pods, sliced crosswise
5. 1 cup cabbage, cut up

The rest

1. One pound beef, chopped into bite-size pieces (half inch or less)
2. 1 Tbs. cooking oil
3. One onion, coarsely chopped
4. One stalk celery, chopped
5. ½ cup dried beans (I like pink beans)
6. 6 cups beef stock (page 27)
7. 1 tsp. *Rice's Beef Enhancer™*
8. 1 tsp. *Rice's Tomato Enhancer™*
9. 1 tsp. salt

Brown the beef in cooking oil. Add onions and celery, cooking until crisp-tender. Add beef stock, beef enhancer, beans, and the puree mix. Cook at low temperature for four hours. Add vegetables, tomato enhancer, salt. Cook for about 45 minutes. Makes about 8 large servings.

Chickeny Vegetable Soup

Use same ingredients and procedures as for the beefy vegetable soup **except:**
1. Use chicken stock, not beef stock
2. Use cooked chicken chunks
3. Use chicken enhancer, not beef enhancer
4. Use only one cup tomatoes
5. Do not brown the chicken; use navy beans

Fresh Tomato Soup

This is a good way to use excess fresh tomatoes. The soup freezes well. Canned tomatoes can be substituted for fresh.

Ingredients
1. 2 Tbs. olive oil
2. 2 medium onions, chopped
3. 4 cups of seeded peeled fresh tomatoes, chopped
4. 2 tsp. *Rice's Tomato Enhancer™*
5. 1 clove garlic, minced
6. 1 Tbs. chopped green chile
7. 2 bay leaves
8. 1 Tbs. fresh parsley
9. 1 tsp. salt
10. 1½ cups milk

Sauté onions in olive oil until translucent. Add tomatoes, garlic, bay leaves, and green chile. Cook over low heat for about 2 hours. Stir occasionally to avoid sticking. Remove bay leaves; add tomato enhancer, fresh parsley, and cook for 30 minutes. For a smooth soup, process in a blender/food processor. For a chunky soup, process half the mixture, and return to the chunky mixture. Add milk and heat almost to boiling. Makes 8 servings.

To freeze:

Freeze soup before adding milk. I usually make a large recipe and freeze in quart zipper plastic bags. To serve frozen soup: thaw, heat to boiling, add milk (one to one and a half cups per quart of soup), heat, and serve.

Cheesy Broccoli Soup

Ingredients:

1. One medium onion, chopped
2. 1 large carrot, peeled and cut into chunks
3. 1 stalk celery, cut into chunks
4. 1 banana pepper, peeled, seeded, and chopped (2 Tbs.)
   Substitute a small bell pepper if needed.
5. 3 Tbs. margarine, oil, or butter
6. 2 Tbs. flour
7. 4 cups chicken stock
8. ½ Tbs. brown sugar
9. ½ tsp. salt
10. ½ tsp. *Rice's Tomato Enhancer™*
11. 2 cups milk
12. 1½ cups shredded American cheese
13. 4 cups chopped fresh broccoli crowns.
14. 1 tsp. lemon juice

Sauté (medium heat) onion, carrot, celery, pepper in melted margarine until the onion turns translucent (about 5 minutes). Add flour and stir into a paste. Gradually add chicken stock and stir to avoid lumps. Add brown sugar, tomato enhancer, and salt. Cook for 45 minutes. Cool slightly and process with a blender or food processor until smooth. Return to the pot. Steam broccoli until it's like you like it. Overcooking affects the bright green color that is so tantalizing in broccoli. Toss with lemon juice. Add cheese to the blended soup and heat until cheese melts. Add milk and broccoli and heat almost to boiling. Makes 8 servings.

> "Steam the broccoli until it's like you like it. Don't destroy the bright green color by overcooking, though."

Bean Soup

Ingredients

1. 1 pound dried beans (lima, black, pinto, ...)
2. 1 medium-large onion
3. 1 large celery stalk
4. 1 large carrot
5. 2 Tbs. oil or butter or margarine
6. 4 cups water
7. 1 tsp. *Rice's Bean Enhancer™*
8. 2 Tbs. chopped lamb's quarters (or cilantro), fresh
9. 1 Tbs. lemon juice
10. 4 cups chicken stock
11. 2 beef bouillon cubes
12. 1 tsp. salt
13. Ham bone or ham hock (optional)

Wash beans, removing any bad ones. Soak beans in the 4 cups water while remainder of ingredients are being prepared. Shred or chop onion, celery, and carrot. Sauté the chopped vegetables in the oil/butter until the onion is translucent. Add all remaining ingredients except salt*. Bring to a boil, and reduce heat to low. Cook covered at low heat for about 4 hours, or until beans are tender. Add salt and cook for another 10 minutes. If a ham bone is used, taste before adding salt. If beans need more liquid along the way, add boiling water. For a thicker stock, remove one cup of the beans and stock and puree in a blender. Add the puree back into the bean soup before serving. Garnish with lemon slices. Makes 8 servings.

* Salt added early-on may make the beans less tender. Also, cold water added during the cooking process may make the beans less tender.

Split Pea Soup

Ingredients

1. 2 cups split peas
2. 2 Tbs. butter/margarine
3. 1 onion
4. 2 cloves garlic
5. 1 carrot, pared or scraped
6. 1 stalk celery
7. 1 tsp. fresh mint (optional)
8. 1 tsp. sugar
9. ½ tsp. salt
10. ½ tsp. *Rice's Bean Enhancer™*
11. 5 cups chicken stock (page 26)
12. 1 cup water
13. 1 cup milk

Mince garlic. Chop onion, carrot, celery, mint to a coarse consistency. Sauté in melted butter/margarine for about 3 minutes. Rinse food processor/chopper with the cup of water, and add to the sautéed vegetables. Add split peas and chicken broth, salt, sugar, bean enhancer. Bring to a boil. Reduce heat to low and cook for about 2 hours, or until peas are tender. For a smooth soup, puree cooked soup in a blender or food processor. I like mine chunky. Add milk and heat almost to boiling. Serve with thin lemon slices as a garnish.

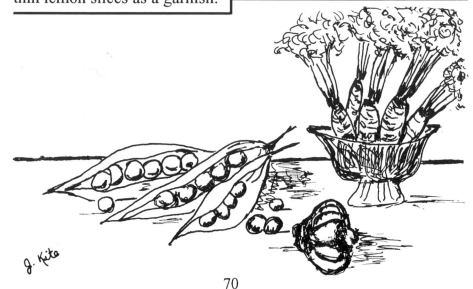

J. Kite

Gumbo

Gumbo is a traditional Cajun soup or stew. To my knowledge, it got its name from the thickening -- which is an okra (gumbo) derivative called filé. It has as its base (stock) a thing called roux. See page 29. Meat additives can be seafood, smoked sausage, chicken, etc.

Ingredients

1. 1 Tbs. olive or peanut oil
2. 1 medium onion, chopped
3. 2 cloves garlic, minced
4. 1 stalk celery, chopped
5. 1 mild pepper, finely chopped (banana or bell)
6. ½ cup of okra, crosscut in half inch slices
7. 1 tsp. Cajun seasoning
8. 1 tsp. *Rice's Seafood Enhancer™*
9. 6 cups roux (page 29)
10. 2 tsp. gumbo filé (optional)
11. ½ cup chopped green onions
12. 2 cups cooked white rice
13. 2 cups raw seafood (shrimp, scallops, oysters, crab, etc.), or cubed chicken, and/or smoked sausage, or a combination.

Heat oil in a Dutch oven or other large pot. Chop ingredients 2-5 in a food processor. Sauté mixture in the oil until the onion is translucent. Add ingredients 6-10 and cook for about an hour. Add meats, and cook about 15 minutes for chicken or smoked sausage; about 5 minutes for seafood. If using a combination of meats, add the seafood about 5 minutes before turning off the burner. Place about ½ cup rice and a proportionate amount of the green onions in each serving bowl. Pour hot gumbo over the rice/green onion and serve. Rice can be used as a side dish as well. Makes about 4-6 servings.

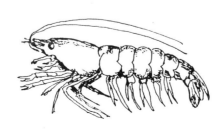

Margaret's Potato Soup

I debated on where to put this recipe. Should it be in the section with Margaret's other recipes -- or should it be with the soups? Soups won out, even though in our family the potato soup specialist is typically woman, not man. Somehow, Margaret's rendition, even with the same ingredients, always turns out better than mine. This is one of those measureless recipes, which can stimulate your creativity.

Ingredients:

1. 4 slices of bacon (or 5 if you snitch one)
2. 3 or 4 medium potatoes
3. 1 medium onion, chopped
4. Milk
5. Water (about half a cup)
6. Salt and pepper to taste
7. Parsley for garnish (optional)

Fry the bacon until crisp. Remove to a paper towel, and retain the grease-- or part of it. Peel the potatoes, and cut into small pieces about a half inch or smaller. Place the onions in bacon grease and cook until translucent. Add potatoes, and mix with the onions. Pour enough milk over the potato mixture to adequately cover the potatoes. Add crumbled bacon. Cook until the potatoes are tender -- about 20 minutes. Using a potato masher or slotted spoon, crush the potatoes to a consistency that you like. Add water, or part of it, if the soup is thicker than you think it should be. Season, garnish with fresh parsley, and serve. Depending on the potato size, the recipe will make 4-6 servings. If you use potatoes from Norway, two servings is about all you will get. My living experience in Norway taught me that Norway probably has the world's smallest potatoes.

> "This is one of those measureless recipes."

Frijoles Charros

A flavorful meal on its own, this soup-like rendition of pinto beans is also a good accompaniment for the NuMex main dishes that follow.

Ingredients

1. 4 slices bacon or 1 Tbs. vegetable oil
2. 1 onion, chopped
3. 1 stalk celery, chopped
4. 2 cloves garlic, minced
5. 1 small Jalapeno pepper, chopped
6. 2 cups dry pinto beans or pink beans
7. 1 ham hock
8. 4 cups water
9. 2 cups chicken stock
10. ½ cup tomatoes and green chiles
11. 4 or 5 sprigs of cilantro, or ½ tsp. dried cilantro
12. 2 tsp. *Rice's Red Herbal Chile Blend™*
13. ½ tsp. salt

Brown bacon and retain grease. Set bacon aside. You can use 1 Tbs. vegetable oil in place of the bacon. Cook the onion, celery, and garlic in the grease/oil until the onion turns translucent. Add crumbled bacon and remaining ingredients except for the salt. Cook over low heat until the beans are tender-about 4 hours. If beans are soaked overnight in the water, cooking time is reduced to about 2 hours. Additional **hot** water can be added along the way to maintain a desired amount of liquid. Remove the ham hock, and add any usable meat back into the soup. If a thicker soup is desired, smash some of the beans with a slotted spoon. Add salt and serve. Makes about 8 servings.

Note: Beans may remain brittle if salt is added early on, or if cold water is added to the beans while they are cooking.

Notes

Chapter 8

<u>NuMex Favorites</u>

Like most folks, I enjoy Mexican cooking. As a youngster, I remember dad bringing home authentic Mexican tamales made with real corn husks. He worked with a Mexican carpenter, and was given tamales and homemade tortillas from time to time. The homemade version always tasted better than the ones from a can. Frozen prepared food was almost nonexistent in those days.

During my high school days, the New Mexico mountains were a favorite retreat. I loved to fly fish for trout and explore the forest trails. We have been regular visitors to New Mexico since then. I remember the New Mexico style enchiladas from Sipapu Lodge almost as clearly as my 17 inch cutthroat trout caught on a fly that I designed myself. I still think those enchiladas are the best that I've ever tasted. The sopapillas were also exceptional. My recipe comes close to duplicating them.

The towns of Dixon, Chimayó, and other villages were in striking distance of the Tres Ritos area (between Mora and Taos) where we stayed. Visits to these villages and towns were like participating in another world. I really enjoyed looking through the grocery stores that had foods that were staples for the local residents -- but were tough to find back home. Those mountain grown chiles were unique; as was the Posole. Fresh fruit was abundant-- apricots in the summer; superb apples in the fall. More sacks of masa harina than flour adorned the shelves. More recently, the raspberry farm at La Cueva came into existence. Besides fresh raspberries, raspberry vinegar is a somewhat unique product. It adds a special touch to spinach salad, my favorite eggplant relish, and a few other dishes. It even complements the herbs and spices in my chili recipe.

One of the most scenic restaurants in the area is Rancho de Chimayó, in the Chimayó, New Mexico area. Traditional New Mexico cuisine is augmented with fajitas, and other specialties. Dining is both inside and outside. The restaurant is always crowded, so reservations are advisable.

My real exposure to NuMex cooking came when we were residents of Los Alamos. A Hispanic colleague who resided in

Truchas brought authentic entrees and accompaniments to work, and shared native recipes and ingredients. I especially remember the flan for dessert. She brought it in a Tupperware covered dish kept in a small portable sized ice chest. She was always a celebrity on flan days. Her sopapillas were also worth waiting for. I've never been able to duplicate these fluffy wonders here in Oklahoma. Maybe it's the lower altitude; then maybe it's just the cook. New Mexico high altitude sopapillas made at Truchas and Sipapu are simply the best ever -- especially when enhanced with high altitude honey.

The fruity meat filling listed in my recipe section was also adapted from this exposure to Hispanic cooking. Whether used to fill tacos, stuff sopapillas, or simply eaten straight out of the skillet, this filling is unique. Perhaps this uniqueness is in part obtained from the fresh fruits grown in the heaven-like setting below the Truchas peaks. I can still picture the beauty of this unique little valley shadowed by the majestic peaks.

I had a superb view of the Truchas peaks out of my office window. Each summer day starting in July, I could almost set my watch by the first cloud that developed over the mountains. About 11:15 AM the first kernel of cloud appeared in precisely the same place. It soon blossomed like a rosebud expanding into full flower. By noon, the blossom had exploded into a full blown cumulous cloud -- then cloned into more. By 2:00 PM, rain, thunder, and lightning were almost always on the horizon. This life giving rain gave special color and flavor to the yellow squash, corn, peppers, and other common ingredients for these special foods. It also gave deep color to the hollyhocks and other flowers, both tame and wild, that painted the village yards and countryside.

Los Alamos Scientific Lab has since given way to the Los Alamos National Laboratory. Another name -- if not another place. Here in this hidden setting that gave birth to the atomic age, other cultures as old as time itself provided innovations whose impact on mankind may exceed the Lab's scientific revelations. The Anasazi people, whose time preceded the American Indians, constructed dwellings, developed a social order, and may have lived in a harmony unknown to modern man.

The Truchas peaks were likely an awe to these people; as they are to us today.

So part of my NuMex cooking expertise is from living the part as a resident. Somehow, food takes on a different air when transported out of the native environment. But even at that, it is a dining experience extraordinare.

NuMex Building Blocks

NuMex Chiles

The "long green chile" is most typically associated with New Mexico cooking. In the grocery stores, the specific chile "breed", the location where it was grown, available moisture, and other factors are usually unknown. The degree of hotness varies to some extent with these factors. For example, seeds planted and grown in Oklahoma will produce different sized and different flavored peppers than the same seed planted in New Mexico. The most common variety is the Anaheim or California chile, which is now grown in many locations besides California.

New Mexico chiles vary from the unnamed varieties that have been grown for centuries across the countryside to named specialties such as **New Mexico #6** and **Big Jim. New Mexico #6** and Anaheim are usually the least hot, while **Big Jim** is typically slightly hotter. These grow quite well here in Oklahoma, and seed is readily available. **Big Jim** makes a good stuffing chile, commonly reaching a foot in length. It is mild enough for most tastes when grown with enough water applied.

In most cases, all green chile varieties can be used interchangeably. When in the Chimayó, New Mexico area, I usually stock up with red chile powder and green chiles when in season. These, in my opinion, have the best flavor of all.

Canned green chiles can be used in most cases as a substitute for fresh roasted green chiles. Fresh roasted green chiles are easier to work with when making chile rellenos.

Red chile is the ripened version of green chile, and is usually found in the grocery in its dried form. Chile (chili) powder is a ground form of dried red chile. Although flavor differs slightly, I usually recommend substituting chile powder for red chile pods due to its ease of use. **One tablespoon of powder averages 2 chile pods.**

Preparing Chiles

The easiest way to prepare chiles is to open a can and pour them out. Nothing smells quite as good as fresh chiles roasting in the oven/broiler or being blistered on the charcoal grill. Fresh roasted chiles are the only way to go for chile rellenos. The canned ones are tooo-o limp to work with. Fresh green chiles from the garden are also less expensive and more fun. They freeze very well. If freezing in bulk, roast but don't peel. I lay them on a cookie sheet, and freeze individually. Then, I place them in a zipper plastic bag. My favorite way to freeze for chopped use is to peel, de-stem and de-seed, then chop. Measure out in 4 oz. (¼ cup) blobs on sprayed foil on a cookie sheet. Freeze and store several individual blobs in a zipper plastic bag.

Now to the roasting. First ingredient is a pair of rubber gloves -- unless you like stinging, burning fingers. Wear the gloves; don't put them on the chiles. Put a small slit in each chile, unless you like explosions in your oven or on your grill. Ovens plastered with chile parts are a mess to clean up. For this reason, and because roasted chile aroma is persistent, I usually heat up the old charcoal grill. Spray the grill with some veggie spray (before the charcoal is fired up). Position the grill about an inch from the coals (if your grill is adjustable). Lay the chiles on the grill and roast until the chile skins blister and turn brown or even a light shade of black. In other words, don't let them stay black very long. Run like sixty into the house to get the tongs that you forgot, and turn the chiles frequently until evenly blistered. Place the chiles in a plastic bag that you remembered to keep handy. Then run like seventy with your plastic bag full of chiles to the freezer, or drop them into a handy ice chest by your grill. In other words, stop the cooking process that will take place in the bag quickly. After the chiles cool enough to peel, grab those rubber gloves and get started. For rellenos, keep the stem intact, use the slit, enlarged if necessary, to remove all the seeds and veins that you can. Freeze whole, or use immediately. For other purposes, remove stems, veins, and seeds. I find that running cold water over the peeled chiles is the best way.

For individual humans who don't want to use a charcoal grill, place the chiles one or two inches under a hot broiler element and process in a similar fashion. If you're a man, be prepared to take a scolding for turning your wife's kitchen into a smelly chile factory.

Other Peppers

Bell peppers, banana peppers, Jalapeno, Poblano, Pasilla, and others round out the list; however, are used in lesser quantities than the green and red chiles.

Pepper blends

Since I enjoy growing many different pepper varieties, I typically peel and mix a blend of banana, chile, Jalapeno, and Poblano. I use about ½ green chile, ¼ banana, and the remaining ¼ whatever else I have. One or two Jalapenos are usually enough. I lay the prepared pods flat, stacked on each other, and freeze on a cookie sheet. I cut the frozen pile into blocks that approximate ¼ cup and place in zipper plastic bags for future use. This mix can be substituted for straight green chile to obtain a more robust flavor.

Tomatillos

Tomatillos grow on a viney plant, and resemble green tomatoes in a husk. The husk is brownish and paper-like. Easy to grow, tomatillos make an interesting garden plant. One or two plants can provide all the tomatillos that you will need, and likely more. Depending on growing conditions, they may reach the size of a golf ball -- but are usually smaller. To use, peel off the husk, and wash off the sticky fluid that covers the fruit. Most recipes use chopped tomatillos either cooked or raw. Tomatillos are unique ingredients for sauces and superb green salsa, imparting a lemony flavor. Store in the husk. Tomatillos can be found in many grocery stores.

Lamb's quarters/Epazote

Also called **epazote** in Spanish, this green plant is used to impart a unique flavor that enhances bean dishes. Mexican epazote looks a little different than the plant that I've seen in Oklahoma. These plants are reported to reduce bean "gas". Also a green that is prepared like spinach, lamb's quarters is difficult to find in the market. It is common in the wild, once you know what to look for. It is reported that sheep will seek it out over other forage. Follow the lamb's advice and try some.

Herbs and Spices

Cilantro, cumin, coriander, oregano, paprika, white pepper, and anise, round out the list of herbs/spices that are common to New Mexico and TexMex cooking. **Cilantro**, preferred over parsley for most NuMex dishes, are the lemony flavored leaves of the coriander plant. **Cumin** (comino) is used in a dry powder form, and is second only to chile in frequency of use. **Coriander** seeds are also used in a ground form. A little coriander goes a long way. **Oregano**, common in Italian cooking, is a staple flavoring for Mexican cuisine. **Paprika** is a ground powder derived from a sweet chile. It is used both as a flavor and garnish. **Anise** seeds impart a licorice flavor to foods; anise is also available as an extract.

Tomatoes

The typical New Mexico tomato form is roasted or broiled. You can often find bits of blackened tomato skins in traditional New Mexico and Texas salsas. From a practical standpoint, I have found that little flavor is sacrificed, and preparation is eased if tomatoes are scalded and peeled. Use canned tomatoes for cooked recipes, especially in place of anemic winter tomatoes.

Other Building Blocks

Tortillas are the bread staple, both in flour and corn forms. Flour tortillas are easy to make, and usually taste better than the packaged varieties. Corn tortillas, on the other hand, require masa harina, and are usually a little bit of trouble to stir up. I typically buy a good brand of prepared corn tortilla to prepare my dishes. There is substantial variation in taste, thickness, and texture among brands, so find one that you like.

> "When roasting chiles - use the charcoal grill, or be prepared to take a scolding for turning your wife's kitchen into a smelly chile factory."

Sauces--Salsas

Sauce or salsa? In the American adaptation to Mexican cuisine, salsas traditionally refer to an appetizer or a garnish, while a sauce usually refers to something that is a basic part of a dish -- for example, enchilada sauce.

Sauces

The key to superb dishes is a superb sauce. The following three sauces are my favorites:

Red Chile Sauce

Ingredients

1. 2 Tbs. olive or vegetable oil
2. ½ cup onions, chopped
3. 2 cloves garlic, minced
4. 1 Tbs. corn starch
5. 2 cups chicken stock
6. ½ cup tomato sauce
7. 3 Tbs. *Rice's Red Herbal Chile Blend™*
8. 2 beef bouillon cubes
9. ½ tsp. salt
10. Scant ¼ tsp. ground cloves

Sauté onions and garlic in oil over medium heat until onions turn limp and translucent - about 3 minutes. Add corn starch and stir until it is absorbed by the oil mixture. Reduce heat to medium low, and gradually add chicken stock, stirring to avoid lumps. Add remaining ingredients, and stir until thoroughly mixed. Simmer for about 15 minutes, stirring occasionally. Makes about 3 cups of sauce.

Variation

For a meaty version, brown about ½ pound of ground beef after sautéing the onions.

Green Chile Sauce

This is a traditional New Mexico green sauce that is used for pork and chicken enchiladas -- and many other dishes. The tomatillos are an addition that gives added flavor, and tones down the "heat" a little.

Ingredients

1. 1 Tbs. olive or vegetable oil
2. ½ cup onions, chopped
3. 2 cloves garlic, minced
4. ¼ cup (4 oz.) chopped green chiles (peeled and de-seeded)
   Use fewer green chiles for a milder sauce.
5. ½ cup tomatillos, chopped
6. 1 Tbs. corn starch
7. 2 cups chicken stock
8. ½ tsp. salt
9. 2 tsp. *Rice's Green Chile Blend™*

Sauté onions and garlic in oil over medium heat until onions turn limp and translucent - about 3 minutes. Add green chiles and tomatillos and stir until well mixed. Add corn starch and stir until it is absorbed by the vegetable mixture. Reduce heat to medium low, and gradually add chicken stock, stirring to avoid lumps. Add remaining ingredients, and stir until thoroughly mixed. Simmer for about 30 minutes, stirring occasionally. Makes about 4 cups of sauce.

Molé Sauce

Pronounced Moh-lay, not like the burrowing garden pest. A traditional Mexican chocolate-chile sauce, it is one of the least common and most flavorful of all. It makes great chicken or beef enchiladas, and can be added to ground beef or chicken as a stuffing for tacos, sopapillas, chile rellenos, and other dishes.

Ingredients

1. ¼ cup vegetable or olive oil
2. 2 medium bell peppers, seeded
3. 1 large onion, quartered
4. 1 stalk celery, cut into large pieces
5. 4 cloves garlic, peeled
6. 3 tomatillos
7. 2 Tbs. sesame seeds
8. 1½ cups chopped tomatoes, fresh or canned (14½ oz. can)
9. 4 Tbs. *Rice's Molé Blend™*
10. 2 cups chicken stock, or a 14½ oz. can of chicken broth
11. ½ tsp. salt
12. 2 tsp. sugar
13. 1 oz. un-sweetened Mexican or other chocolate
14. ½ cup pecans or almonds, toasted at 300°F for 15 minutes

Chop items 2-6 to a medium texture in a food processor. Add sesame seeds, and sauté the mixture in the oil for about 5 minutes at medium heat, stirring frequently. Before adding chocolate, see variations below. Add remaining ingredients in the order listed, except for the nuts. Simmer for 30 minutes or more over low heat. Chop nuts, and add to the mixture. Makes about 5 cups of sauce. Freeze any excess and use later.

Variations

I prefer a sauce that has a little less chocolate than is typical for this recipe. Start with ½ oz. of chocolate, taste, and add part or all of the remainder depending on your taste preference. If you're a real chile-chocoholic, add even more chocolate -- up to 2 ounces.

Salsas

Salsas have become a traditional part of Mexican cuisine. Most American restaurants that serve Mexican dishes start with tortilla chips and salsa-- that is, red salsa. Some areas of the USA offer both red and green salsas, but red (tomato based) salsa is far more common. Green salsa recipes are few and far between. Salsas are typically an "add-on" , rather than an intrinsic part of an entree.

Green Salsas

The base ingredient for green salsa is the tomatillo, described in **NuMex Building Blocks.** Avocado, onion, spices, and occasionally green tomatoes find their way into salsa verde.

Red Salsas

There are literally hundreds of red salsa recipes. Although the ingredients are similar, the individual portions are variable. There are fresh red salsas; there are cooked red salsas. Some are smooth; some are chunky. The degree of "picante" varies from mild to very hot. My advice is to search the grocer's shelves till you find one or more that suit your taste.

Perhaps an exception is salsa made from fresh ingredients. If you have lots of tomatoes, peppers, onions, and spices in the garden, why spend good money on the bottled stuff? Also, fresh red salsa offers a change of pace -or maybe that's **Pace**®. The following recipe is a standard basic fresh tomato based recipe. Feel free to modify it until it suits your level of "heat" and taste. Also, authentic Mexican red salsas may use roasted tomatoes. If roasted tomatoes are used, the resulting salsa often contains bits of blackened tomato skins. Roast your tomatoes under the broiler element until the skins are blackened, or immerse them in boiling water for a half minute or so. Remove the peels.

Fresh Red Salsa

Ingredients

1. 2 strips bacon (optional)
2. 1 Tbs. vegetable oil
3. 2 cloves garlic
4. 1 medium onion, quartered
5. 1 banana or ½ bell pepper, seeded
6. 2 Tbs. roasted green chile, more or less to taste
7. 1 small Jalapeno pepper, seeded
8. A dozen or so sprigs of cilantro
9. 2 tsp. *Rice's Green Chile Blend™*
10. 1 cup (8 oz.) tomato sauce
11. 1 tsp. salt (more or less to your taste)
12. 1 additional medium raw onion, chopped.
13. 3 cups fresh peeled seeded tomatoes
14. Juice from one or two limes (about 2 Tbs.)
15. 1 Tbs. Wine vinegar (I prefer red)
16. 1 Tbs. Raspberry vinegar (or other vinegar)
17. 1 tsp. sugar

Brown the bacon until crisp, retaining the drippings. Eat the bacon or discard it. Also, dogs love bacon. Add vegetable oil. Mince garlic, and add other ingredients (4-8) a few at a time through the food chute of a food processor - or otherwise chop. Sauté the chopped ingredients (3-8), green chile blend, tomato sauce, and salt for about 3 minutes over medium heat. Don't overcook. Place the remaining ingredients in the food processor bowl and chop until the mixture reaches a desired consistency. Add the sautéed mixture, blend well, and serve. Flavor is improved if the salsa is refrigerated for several hours to let the flavors commingle.

Again, these are the ingredients and proportions that I like. Feel free to experiment with these ingredients and flavorings until you find a combination that suits your taste.

Salsa Verde (Green Salsa)

Most tomatillo based recipes that I've seen use cooked tomatillos. I like this adaptation that uses raw ingredients. A food processor is almost essential for this recipe. This salsa is similar to green salsas offered by restaurants in the Houston area.

Ingredients

1. 2 cloves garlic
2. 1½ cups (approx.) tomatillos, husked, washed and halved
3. 1 small onion, peeled and quartered
4. 2-3 sprigs of cilantro
5. 1 avocado, pared and seeded
6. Juice from one lime
7. 1 small Jalapeno, seeded (less for a milder salsa)
8. 2 tsp. *Rice's Green Chile Blend™*
9. ½ tsp. sugar. (optional)
10. ¼ cup sour cream

Mince the garlic in your food processor. Add tomatillos, cilantro, and onion and chop until almost a liquid form. Add avocado and lime. Blend until smooth. Add remaining ingredients and blend for a minute or so. Serve with tortilla chips, or use as a garnish.

"This salsa verde may turn your friends green with envy!"

Fillings

Whether for enchiladas, tacos, or other similar fare (even stuffed sopapillas), fillings can be served with a variety of sauces to make many unique dishes.

Fruity Meat Filling

This is one of the most unique fillings that I've tasted. Use it in enchiladas, tacos, stuffed sopapillas, chile rellenos -- or eat it with tortilla chips. I've even eaten it straight out of the pan.

Ingredients

1. 2 Tbs. peanut or other vegetable oil
2. 1 lb. ground beef
3. 1 onion, chopped
4. 3 tomatoes, or 1 cup drained canned tomatoes, chopped
5. ½ cup raisins
6. 1 cup total -apples, pears, pineapple, or combination, chopped
7. ¼ cup chopped green chiles (or less)
8. ½ cup seedless grapes, chopped
9. 1 tsp. salt
10. 1½ tsp. *Rice's Molé Blend™*
11. 1½ tsp. *Rice's Red Herbal Chile Blend™*
12. ½ cup chopped pecans, toasted at 300 degrees for 15 min.

Soak raisins in warm water for 10 minutes. Discard the juice. Sauté onions in oil for about 3 minutes at medium heat. Add ground beef, and brown. Add remaining ingredients, except for the pecans. Cook for 30 minutes at low heat, stirring occasionally. Add pecans, and use immediately as a taco filling, enchilada filling, etc.

Vegetable Filling

The listed veggies are my favorites for this dish, except I like to replace about ¼ of the spinach with lamb's quarters. Use any vegetables that you like to yield 2½ cups.

1. 1 cup cooked spinach, well drained
2. ½ cup mushrooms
3. ½ cup zucchini
4. ½ cup onion
5. 1 clove garlic
6. 1 Tbs. olive or vegetable oil
7. ½ cup bread crumbs
8. 2 tsp. *Rice's Molé Blend™*
9. 1 egg
10. ½ cup half and half, or plain yogurt, or sour cream
11. ¼ cup Monterey Jack or Mozzarella Cheese, grated
12. ½ tsp. salt

Place the spinach in a colander and press out as much water as possible. A food processor is handy for shredding or chopping the veggies. Mince the garlic, and in the same processor bowl shred or coarsely chop (about pea size) items 2-4. Sauté the vegetables in the oil for about 5 minutes. Add the spinach, and mix until the spinach is blended with the other ingredients. Add remaining ingredients, and stir until thoroughly mixed. Chill until ready to use.

Beef Filling

Ingredients

1. ½ pound ground beef
2. 2 Tbs. chopped onion
3. 1 tsp. *Rice's Red Herbal Chile Blend™*
4. 2 Tbs. red salsa or other tomato additive, and enough water to make ¼ cup.
5. ¼ tsp. salt

Brown ground beef. Add onion, stir, then cook for about two minutes. Add items 3, 4, and 5. Cook until the liquid is absorbed.

Chicken Filling

1. ½ cup shredded onion
2. 1 small carrot, shredded
3. 2 cloves garlic, minced
4. ½ cup sauce *
5. ½ cup shredded Monterey Jack cheese
6. 1 Tbs. olive or vegetable oil
7. ½ cup sour cream
8. ½ cup half and half, or plain yogurt
9. 2 cups cooked shredded chicken
10. 2 tsp. *Rice's Green Chile Blend™*
11. 1 Tbs. fresh cilantro, chopped
12. ½ tsp. salt

   *   Use sauce recipes on pages 82-84, or your own.

Sauté onion, garlic, and carrot in the oil until the onion becomes translucent. Add chicken, sauce, cilantro, salt, and green chile blend. Cook over low heat for 20 minutes. Add sour cream, half and half (or yogurt), and stir over low heat until well mixed. Chill until used.

Cheese and Onion Filling

1. 1 cup shredded longhorn or other cheddar cheese
2. 1 cup shredded white cheese (Monterey Jack, Swiss, etc.)
3. 1 medium onion, chopped
4. 2 tsp. cooking oil
5. 1 tsp. *Rice's Red Herbal Chile Blend™*

Sauté onion in oil for about a minute. Add red chile blend. Stir until onion is coated. Remove from heat and let cool for two to three minutes. Stir in cheeses. Cheeses should soften, but not melt. Use immediately.

Enchiladas

The traditional New Mexico enchiladas are stacked, not rolled as one usually sees in the TexMex style. I like the stacked option best, but the taste is probably the same since ingredients and basic preparation are common to both methods. An added touch to the New Mexico tradition is an egg on top of the stack.

The three sauces described earlier can be used in combination with fillings made from different meats, cheeses, and vegetables to make a whole array of enchilada dishes.

Basic preparation - stacked enchiladas

1. Prepare the sauce.
2. Prepare the filling.
3. Dip corn tortillas (3 per serving) in hot oil to limber them.
4. Dip tortillas individually in the sauce (cover completely).
5. Place the first tortilla on the bottom of the baking dish or on a oven-proof plate.
6. Add filling to thinly cover the prepared tortilla.
7. Add remaining tortillas and fillings in sequence.
8. Add about ¼ cup of sauce over the top of the stack.
9. Cover and bake for about 15 minutes until thoroughly hot.
10. Optionally add a cooked egg to the top of the stack.
11. Garnish with chopped fresh tomato, chopped onion, etc.

Basic preparation - rolled enchiladas

Steps are essentially the same, except that the filling is placed in the center of the tortilla, and then each tortilla is rolled. Place the seam on the bottom of the baking dish or oven-proof plate. Add sauce to cover the rolled enchiladas, and bake as above. A serving is typically two enchiladas.

Chile Rellenos

Perhaps the most unique of the Mexican foods, chile rellenos are not easy to make. Don't expect perfect rellenos the first time you try to assemble them. In my opinion, canned chiles are almost impossible to work with. This recipe calls for fresh roasted long green chiles (Anaheim, Big Jim, etc.) These chiles are typically available all year in most grocery stores. Of course, you can grow your own; peel and stuff; then freeze for later use.

Ingredients

1. 6 roasted and peeled green chiles, stems intact
2. 3 eggs
3. 3 Tbs. flour
4. ¼ tsp. salt
5. Filling (see below), about 2-3 Tbs. per chile-depending on size.
6. ½ cup flour
7. ¼ tsp. salt
8. Oil for frying

Prepare the chiles

Cut a slit in each chile, starting at the stem end and continuing about half the length of the chile. Sometimes, the slit will extend itself to the end. (at least that's what I tell myself). Clean out the seeds best as you can. I carefully rinse mine under a small stream of cold water. Place the filling inside the chile, and close. Don't worry if a little filling shows through. These peeled, stuffed chiles can be frozen, and thawed at a later time to complete the relleno preparation. I usually make a big batch and freeze some for later use.

Fillings (see pages 88-90)

Use cheese and onion filling, beef filling, or fruity meat filing. Some recipes specify filling the relleno with small cubes of Monterey jack and/or cheddar cheese, with or without chopped onion.

Continued on next page

Chile Rellenos, Continued

Relleno assembly and preparation

Combine items 6 and 7 and dump the mixture onto wax paper. Carefully, roll, dust- whatever, to coat the chile with the flour/salt mix. Prepare all chiles before continuing.

Beat the eggs for about three minutes at high speed. Add flour and salt (items 3,4) gradually, and beat slowly until the flour is absorbed -- a minute or less, making a batter. Heat about a half inch of oil in a skillet. Coat the chile with batter, and using a spatula, carefully place the chile into the hot oil. If necessary, add some batter to the top of the chile, spreading to cover. Spoon hot oil over the chile until sealed. Turn the chile to brown best as you can on all sides. Serve with your favorite chile con queso (chile-cheese sauce), or the tomato sauce listed below.

Other options

Batter. Some recipes call for separating the egg yolks from the whites. The egg yolks are beaten with the flour, and the stiffly beaten whites are then folded into the yolk/flour mixture. This option results in a puffier coating for the relleno.

Frying. Chile Rellenos can be fried in a deep fryer; however, I find the skillet method more convenient.

Tomato Sauce

Ingredients

1. 1 Tbs. vegetable oil
2. 1 small onion, about ½ cup
3. Tomatoes and green chiles(10-15 oz. can)
4. 2 cloves garlic, minced
5. ½ tsp. sugar
6. ½ tsp. *Rice's Green Chile Blend™.*
7. Salt to taste
8. 5-6 sprigs chopped fresh cilantro
9. 8 oz. can of tomato sauce (optional)

Sauté onion in oil until translucent - about 3 minutes. Add remaining ingredients and simmer over low heat for 20 minutes or more. Add canned tomato sauce if desired.

Flour Tortillas

Freshly made flour tortillas are easy, and certainly worth the trouble. They can be made to virtually any size within reason, but are commonly about 7 inches in diameter. The main things to remember are to not overwork the dough, and to use hot, but not boiling water. Let the dough season for about 30 minutes in a plastic bag, or covered dish.

Ingredients

1. 2 cups flour
2. 1½ tsp. salt
3. 1 tsp. baking powder
4. ¼ tsp. sugar
5. 3/4 cup hot water
6. ¼ cup flour
7. 4 Tbs. shortening (lard is the historic ingredient)

Combine dry ingredients. Cut in shortening with a pastry blender. Add in water, and stir to make a dough. If the dough is sticky, add part or all of the additional ¼ cup flour a little at a time until the dough is stiff and not sticky. Knead the dough several times, and let stand for about a half hour (see first paragraph). Form balls about golf ball size, or larger for king size tortillas. Roll out into approximate circles on a floured board or wax paper. If you wipe the working surface under the wax paper with a damp rag, the wax paper won't slide around. Cook about a minute or less on each side on a preheated griddle or pan sprayed slightly with a cooking spray. Blisters will form on the top side when ready to turn. Makes about a dozen average size tortillas. Cooked tortillas can be frozen and reheated, or raw tortillas can be frozen, thawed, and cooked.

Sopapillas

The first and best Sopapillas that I ever ate were at the Sipapu Lodge near Tres Ritos, New Mexico. I remember my nephew, who was about 5 at the time, as he was introduced to sopapillas. A somewhat finicky eater, he believed in eating one thing at a time. I think he even ate his bread and then ate the jelly separately. His "sofa pillows" and honey were eaten by taking a bite of sopapilla, then a spoonful of honey. At least it was less messy that way. I always manage to dribble a little, or sometimes a lot of honey onto my shirt as a standard part of the sopapilla ritual.

Ingredients:

1. 2 cups flour
2. 2 tsp. baking powder
3. ½ tsp. sugar
4. 1½ tsp. salt
5. 2 Tbs. shortening
6. 3/4 cup hot water
7. ¼ cup flour

Combine dry ingredients 1- 4. Cut in shortening with a pastry blender. Add hot water and stir to form a dough. If the dough is sticky, add part or all of the ¼ cup of flour until the dough is easy to work with. Knead the dough several times, and let stand in a plastic bag or covered bowl for half an hour. Roll out the dough to about an eighth of an inch thick, keeping it in the form of an approximate rectangle. Wipe the top side of the dough with a slightly damp rag, and fold the dough in half. Let stand for about 5 minutes. Roll the dough again until it's about an eighth of an inch thick. Cut into 3 inch squares, roll again if necessary, and fry one at a time at 375 degrees. Oil should be at least two inches deep. Spoon the oil over the top of the sopapilla to encourage puffing. After about two minutes, turn the sopapilla over and cook for an additional minute or so. Drain on paper towels. Makes about a dozen. Optionally, sprinkle with a cinnamon and sugar mix. Serve with honey.

Fruity Meat Tacos

Fruity meat filling provides a different taste from the conventional beef or chicken filling. Many tacos are made with ready-made taco shells. Simply fill the folded ready-made shells about half full with the meat filling. Optionally, place in an oven preheated to 350°F for about 5 minutes. Then add grated cheese, shredded lettuce, chopped tomatoes, and you're done.

Another approach is to warm fresh tortillas on a grill or in a skillet until limp, then stuff with filling. Fold the taco shell to look like the store-bought ready mades. Secure the two ends with a toothpick, wooden of course, and fry in oil for about a minute. Turn and repeat the other side for the same uno minuto. When cooled enough to touch, add cheese, lettuce, and chopped tomatoes. Soft tacos are made in a similar fashion, but the frying is omitted.

Posole

Posole is a pork and hominy stew that serves as a staple for many New Mexico families. There are many adaptations and variations in the ingredients. In my opinion, frozen posole works better than the dry version, or canned hominy. Frozen posole is hard to find outside New Mexico. For people who hate hominy, substitute white beans in equal portions.

1. 1 cup frozen posole, dry posole, or two cups canned hominy
2. 1 pound cubed pork
3. 1 Tbs. vegetable oil or other fat
4. 1 onion, chopped
5. ½ cup chopped celery
6. 1 carrot, chopped
7. 2 cloves garlic, minced
8. ½ cup chopped bell pepper
9. 4 cups chicken broth
10. 1 Tbs. *Rice's Green Chile Blend™*
11. 2 Tbs. Pasilla chili pepper (substitute 1 Tbs. chili powder if you can't find Pasilla pepper)
12. ½ tsp. salt, or to taste.

Brown the pork in oil. Add celery, pepper, and onion, Cook until the onion is translucent. Add chicken broth and remaining ingredients. Cook over low heat until the posole has softened - about 3 hours.

Flan (Caramel Custard)

A traditional Mexican dessert, flan is hard to pass up. One smell, one taste, and your diet is due for a crash. This recipe uses whole eggs and produces a lighter custard than recipes that recommend both eggs and egg yolks. **Start early.** Flan needs to cool for about 2 hours before serving.

The caramel

1. 1 cup sugar
2. ½ cup water

Combine sugar and water in a saucepan. Heat and stir until sugar dissolves. Proceed to cook without stirring over medium heat until the sugar caramelizes (turns an amber color). Remove from heat and pour quickly into separate custard cups, or a loaf pan. Tilt and swirl the cup/pan so that the caramel coats the bottom and part of the sides.

The custard

1. 5 large eggs
2. ½ cup sugar
3. One 13 oz. can evaporated milk
4. 1½ cups milk
5. 2 tsp. vanilla, amaretto, or other flavoring.
6. Dash of salt

Preheat oven to 350°F. Combine milks, sugar, and salt in a saucepan. Over low heat, stir the mixture until sugar dissolves. Continue to heat until steam starts to rise--just before the mixture boils. Beat the eggs at low speed for about a minute until whites and yolks are thoroughly mixed. Beat about half the warm milk mixture into the eggs, add vanilla, then beat in the other half. Pour custard into loaf pan or cups, and place the filled containers in a water-filled pan. Cover with a cookie sheet or foil for a better texture. Bake for an hour and 15 minutes, or until a knife inserted into the custard comes out clean. **Very important:** Let the flan cool for two hours. If you don't, the caramel will stick to the bottom of the cups or loaf pan. Loosen the edges with a knife, and invert the cups/loaf onto serving dishes/platter. Serves about 10, so you can half the recipe if you want a smaller batch.

Chapter 9

Nutty Delights

As a pecan grower and author of a book on pecans, nuts (especially pecans) have always been a favorite recipe ingredient. Nuts provide unique flavors and textures that enhance foods of many types. This section deals with dessert foods, although nuts are essential ingredients in several other recipes included throughout this book's pages. Almonds in the spinach salad, toasted pecans in the fruity meat filling, and more. A little dab of nuts tastes good in almost any fruit cobbler, and offers a pleasant surprise if added to almost any recipe.

Mumpsy the squirrel. With a nut in their mouth pouch, squirrels appear to have a severe case of the mumps. Experts in nut removal, squirrels can empty a tree quickly.

Choco-nutaholic Cookies

Ingredients:

1. ½ cup shortening
2. ½ cup of butter (or other favorite butter substitute)
3. 1 cup sugar
4. 1 cup brown sugar
5. 2 eggs
6. ¼ tsp. saffron (optional)
7. 1 tsp. vanilla
8. 2 cups all purpose flour
9. 1 tsp. soda
10. ½ tsp. salt
11. 1 tsp. baking powder
12. 2½ cups blenderized oatmeal (see below)
13. 12 oz. pkg. genuine chocolate chips
14. 4 oz. of chocolate bar, grated, or white chocolate, grated
15. 1¼ cup crumbled pecans
16. ¼ cup black walnuts (optional)

If using saffron, add saffron to eggs and stir. Set aside. Cream both sugars, shortening, butter. Add eggs and vanilla. Mix in flour, blenderized oatmeal, salt, soda, baking powder - until thoroughly moistened. Add in the chocolates and nuts. Stir thoroughly. Roll into one inch balls and place about 2 inches apart on a cookie sheet. Bake for 11 minutes at 375 degrees. Cool and eat (or eat without cooling -- chocolate can burn your mouth, but fresh hot cookies may be worth the risk). This recipe makes about 4 dozen cookies unless you eat too much raw cookie dough.

Blenderized Oatmeal;

Measure oatmeal and blend in a blender until it turns to a fine powder. Foodprocessorized oatmeal also works.

Nutty options:

If you can find hican nuts, they add a special nutty flavor. Replace ¼ cup of the pecans with hicans (a hickory and pecan cross). Also, omit the black walnuts if you can't find any.

Pineanna Nut Muffins

Ingredients:

1. 1 cup whole wheat flour
2. 1 cup quick oats
3. ½ cup all purpose flour
4. ¼ cup sugar
5. ¼ cup brown sugar
6. ¼ cup wheat germ
7. 1½ tsp. baking soda
8. ½ tsp. salt
9. 1 tsp. cinnamon
10. 2 eggs, slightly beaten
11. ½ cup crushed pineapple
12. 1 cup smashed bananas, peeled of course
13. ¼ cup veggie oil
14. 2 Tbs. butter or margarine, softened
15. ½ cup crumbled pecans
16. 2 Tbs. chopped black walnuts
17. 1/3 cup raisins (optional)

Combine and mix ingredients 1-9 in a mixing bowl. (Or a combining bowl). Set aside. Combine ingredients 10-14 and mix for a minute or so at slow speed with a mixer or by hand. Add dry ingredient mixture and stir until moistened. Add pecans and walnuts and stir until these essential ingredients enhance every nook and cranny of the muffin batter. Add raisins if it suits your taste. Place batter into muffin cups, filling almost to the top. Bake in a preheated oven at 350°F for precisely 22 minutes, or precisely for 21 minutes -- or maybe 21½ minutes, or until they look done. Makes about 16 muffins.

Serve with honey butter made with equal parts honey and butter / margarine.

"What in the world is a pineanna?"

Recipes/food facts from: <u>Pecans--A Grower's Perspective</u>

Selecting Pecans

Packaged kernels- Choose pecans that are straw colored and bright. Dull and dark colored kernels may be old and rancid. Full bodied pecans that show a solid cross section typically have superior flavor. Although some pecan varieties may produce kernels that are naturally amber in color, it is difficult to distinguish freshness without a taste test. Kernels should snap when broken, but should not shatter. Excessive crumbling/shattering indicates excessive dryness. Pecans that bend without breaking contain excessive moisture.

In-shell pecans- Choose pecans that are clean and free of cracks in the shell. An oily shell exterior may indicate lack of freshness. The best way to distinguish fresh in-shell pecans is to crack open a few to examine the kernels. Use the same criteria mentioned above in kernels. Percent kernel varies from less than 40% to about 60%, depending on variety. Typically, the thinner the shell- the higher percent of edible kernel. Some pecans are easier to extract from the shell than others. This property can also be estimated by cracking a few pecans. Until you gain some experience in recognizing superior varieties, purchase a few for evaluation before buying a bunch.

Natives-vs.-papershells- Papershell is a name often given to improved variety pecans. Papershells are typically larger and have thinner shells than their native counterparts. It is usually far easier and quicker to extract a cup of kernels from paper shell pecans than from the typically smaller natives. On the other hand, native pecans may have higher oil content and better overall quality when compared with some papershell varieties. Personally, I like the smaller native kernels for pecan pie, and some other recipes that call for pecan halves. Average natives shell out at 40% kernel while papershells usually yield 50-60% edible meat. Keep this in mind when evaluating price per pound.

Recipes

Honey Pecan Pie

No, this is not pecan pie made by Honey or for Honey; the pie has honey in it. For a traditional pecan pie, use corn syrup in place of the honey.

Ingredients:

1. 4 eggs, slightly beaten
2. ½ cup of honey
3. ½ cup light corn syrup
4. 1 cup of sugar
5. 1/3 cup butter or margarine, melted
6. ¼ tsp. salt
7. 1 tsp. vanilla or bourbon
8. 1¼ cups pecans

Combine the first 7 ingredients and mix well, but not to the point that it is frothy. Add pecans and stir until the pecans are coated. Pour into an uncooked pastry shell and bake in a preheated oven at 350°F for approximately 55 minutes.

Pastry shell:

1. 1¼ cups of flour
2. ½ tsp. salt
3. ½ cup shortening or margarine
4. 2 Tbs. cold water

Mix salt and flour. Using a pastry blender, cut shortening into the flour mix until it resembles coarse meal. Add water, stirring with a fork or spoon until thoroughly moistened. Form a ball with the dough and roll out on floured waxed paper. Place the dough in a 9 inch pie plate and prepare the edges to your liking. Use extreme care not to put any holes in the dough, or the filling will run under the crust.

Pecan Nougat Bars

Ingredients:

1. 2/3 cup vegetable oil
2. 2 cups brown sugar
3. 2 eggs
4. 1 tsp. vanilla
5. 1 cup pecans
6. 1 cup chocolate chips
7. 1½ cups flour
8. 2 tsp. baking powder
9. ¼ tsp. salt

Combine ingredients in the order listed, mix until moistened. Bake in a greased cake pan at 350°F for 25 minutes. (Courtesy of Jean Hoffman, Stillwater, Oklahoma)

Roasted Pecans

Ingredients:

1. 2 cups of pecan halves
2. ½ tsp. salt
3. 2 Tbs. butter or margarine

Melt margarine or butter, taking care not to scorch. Add salt and stir over low heat for a few minutes. Add pecans and stir until the pecans are coated. Spread out in a single layer on a foil lined shallow baking sheet and cook at 300° F for thirty minutes. Additional salt can be added during the baking process if desired. Cool and serve.

Pecan Yummy Bars

Base:
1. 3 Tbs. brown sugar
2. ½ cup butter or margarine
3. 1 cup flour
4. ¼ cup finely chopped pecans

Combine ingredients and pat into a 9 Inch square baking pan. Bake at 350° for 15 minutes. Remove from oven to cool slightly.

Filling:
1. 2 eggs
2. 1 cup brown sugar
3. ½ cup granulated sugar
4. ½ tsp. baking powder
5. ½ tsp. vanilla
6. 1¼ cups coarsely chopped pecans

Combine first five ingredients and mix at slow speed or by hand for about a minute. Add pecans and stir until coated. Pour over base. Bake at 350°F for 25 minutes. Cool for several hours. Cut into squares or bars and serve.

Pecans Caliente

1. 2 Tbs. butter or margarine
2. 2 Tbs. soy sauce
3. 1 to 3 shakes of hot sauce
4. ½ tsp. salt
5. 1 tsp. honey
6. 2 cups of pecan halves

Combine first 5 ingredients in a small saucepan. Heat until butter or margarine is melted. Add pecans and stir until the pecans are coated. Bake for 30 minutes at 300° F, stirring occasionally. Additional salt and hot sauce can be added during the cooking process. Cool and serve.

Caliente means h-o-ttt !!

Pecan Pralines

Ingredients:

1. 1½ cups sugar
2. 3/4 cup brown sugar, packed
3. 6 Tbs. butter or margarine
4. ½ cup half and half
5. 1½ cups coarsely chopped pecans
6. 1 tsp. vanilla

Spray about 2 ft. of waxed paper with vegetable spray. Set aside. Combine all ingredients except vanilla in a heavy saucepan. Bring to a boil, stirring constantly. Boil uncovered over medium heat, stirring constantly, to the soft ball stage (candy thermometer reads 220°F). Remove from heat. After cooling for two or three minutes, add vanilla and beat with a wooden spoon for about 5 minutes, or until mixture starts to thicken. Working quickly, drop onto sprayed waxed paper using the wooden spoon or a serving spoon . Makes about 2 dozen pralines.

Pecan Double Fudge Brownies

Ingredients:
1. 1 cup sugar
2. ½ cup butter or margarine, softened
3. 2 eggs
4. 3 Tbs. Cocoa
5. 3/4 cup flour
6. ½ tsp. baking soda
7. ¼ tsp. salt
8. 1 tsp. rum or vanilla
9. ½ cup semisweet chocolate chips
10. (Optional) 2 cups of small marshmallows
11. ½ cup pecans

Frosting:
1. 3 oz. cream cheese, softened
2. 1 Tbs. margarine, softened
3. 2 cups powdered sugar
4. 1-2 Tbs. milk or cream
5. 4 Tbs. cocoa

For brownies:

Cream sugar and butter or margarine at medium speed with an electric mixer. Add eggs separately, beating for a minute after each one. Combine ingredients 4-7, and add to creamed mixture. Mix slowly for about a minute. Stir in chocolate chips, vanilla, and pecans. Pour resulting mixture into a greased and floured 9 inch square baking pan. Bake at 350°F for 25 minutes. Remove from oven. Add marshmallows and cover with foil or a baking sheet until marshmallows melt. Cool and spread frosting. Makes 24-30 brownies.

For frosting:

Combine 1 Tbs. cream or milk, margarine, cocoa, and cream cheese in a mixing bowl. Beat slowly until ingredients are blended, then beat at medium speed for a minute. Add powdered sugar and stir or beat slowly until blended. Beat at medium speed until the frosting is smooth. Add up to 1 Tbs. additional milk or cream for a desired consistency.

<u>Notes</u>

Chapter 10

Smokery & Barbecue Cooking

In the beginning, man obviously determined that cooked meat, and certain vegetables tasted a lot better than the raw stuff. As such, man first cooked these things over an open fire. Where there's fire there's almost always smoke. So man's first cooking attempts had smoky flavor as a part of the natural process. I guess he learned to like it.

Since then -with man's ingenuity- he has fancied up the art and science of smokery cooking. He has engineered the art and science of a thing called the smoker. It may have electric elements, water pans, thermometers, stainless steel innards, and other such complexities. My smoker needs outriggers to keep the dog from jumping up and knocking the whole shootin' match over. It's amazing that a dog will brave both fire and the master's wrath to grab a smoked brisket. How can one dog eat a whole brisket?? Ask mine to find out. I just wish she would clean up the water and rest of the mess after she finishes woofing down the meat.

Man, in his infinite wisdom, has discovered that some woods flavor meat and other edibles better than other woods. He also learned that one way to get rid of old herb stems and other leftover parts is to burn them. It gets rid of those unsightly things, and adds a nice aroma to whatever the smoke comes in contact with. Blue jeans, T-shirts, baseball hats, etc., smell almost good enough to eat. Any meat or veggies cooking are also similarly enhanced.

Woods in the woods vary with geographical area. Vine maple, a good smoking wood, exists in the Pacific Northwest -- and probably other places. The same with alder. Good woods for smoking! Hickory and pecan are abundant in parts of the Midwest and South. They do a reputable job of flavoring meats. I thought persimmon might make a good smoking wood. I thought wrong. I didn't think hackberry would enhance anything. I was wrong again. Mesquite is a nuisance in the Southwest, but it is great for cooking. Add them all together, and the neighbors may beat a path to your door, scale your seven foot fence-- or steal the brisket out of your smoker, in spite of themselves. They may even train their dog to fetch your smoked turkey accidentally on purpose. Bird dogs, I think they call them. Just joking of course.

The art and science of smokery cooking is relatively easy. A few good herbs and wood chips; a good smoker; a few secret marinades; things to smoke-- and you're off.

> Note: The low temperatures involved in smoking meats/ other foods may increase the risk of food poisoning. **Follow the instructions provided with your smoker.** Use a meat thermometer to ensure that the meat is done. Prior to smoking, some meats are typically cured with mixes that may have food preservatives included. Always keep meats and other perishable foods refrigerated until ready to cook, and return them to the refrigerator soon after your meal.

The Smoker

Smokers come in all sizes and price ranges. Some have water pans; others don't. Some family sized apparatus can set you back a thousand dollars or more. Other suitable ones can be had for less than a hundred. A superb brisket can be created from the $60.00 variety; a lousy brisket can come from one of those four figure jobs. Quality is derived from good meat, good marinades, good woods and herbs, and adequate time.

I like a smoker that has a water pan, an electric element, and a way to burn a little wood and herbs for smoke. A total wood burning variety also works, but you need to spend more time watching and feeding it. I like to start my brisket in the morning, add water at noon, and take the finished product off the smoker for dinner. In the mean time, I can be off doing other fun stuff. Grafting pecan trees, fishing, and gardening are all more fun than watching a smoker. Besides, I can take the dog with me and lessen the chances of losing a brisket along the way.

The Wood

In our neck of the woods, abundant pecan and hackberry exist. Throw in a little mesquite from my kinfolk in the Texas Panhandle, Midland, and Abilene, and I've got what I need. I even checked some vine maple logs in a gunny sack as airplane luggage once all the way from Oregon. That event got almost as many stares as my checking a roll of irrigation tubing. Fruit woods such as apple have a decent aroma when burned, but I like pecan, etc. better. Hickory, of which pecan is a member, is of course a reliable standard. Oaks generally burn hot, but have little aroma and flavor to contribute. For some reason, pecan is my favorite. Avoid pine and other woods with a high tar content.

The Herbs

Save those overgrown herb stems; the stuff that will not go through the colander; and other herby things. If they're dry, soak them in a little water to make the herbal fire experience last a little longer. It also minimizes the opportunity to singe your eyebrows. The smell of burning eyebrows even out does the smell of burning basil stems.

Rosemary is perhaps my favorite herb for smoking. I usually add it irregardless of the meat that I'm cooking. Sage is nice for poultry. Thyme, oregano, and basil are also good flavor enhancers for most anything. Tarragon is nice for fish and other seafood. I usually avoid parsley and cilantro; they don't appeal to me when burned.

Other Stuff for the Fire

Brown sugar adds a nice color and flavor when burned. I place brown sugar in aluminum foil, fold it a few times, and poke a few holes in the top. You can also add some herbs in the packet, if you want to. Lay it on the fiery part of the smoker, but avoid getting it on the electric elements. Aluminum foil can ignite with a bright flash, becoming a hazard to both you and your smoker.

The Art and Science of Smoking Meats

Wood and herbal smoke impart a unique flavor to meats. The outside layer of smoked meats also develops a distinct color (a reddish tint), due to the interaction of smoke carbon particles with meat pigments. The surface meat also coagulates, due to the interaction of the meat surface with acids emitted by the smoke. These acids help to prevent formation of mold and bacterial agents--a most important property before the days of refrigeration.

Temperatures

Temperatures may vary, depending on your smoker. Follow the guidelines included with your smoking equipment. According to my smoker instructions, smoked meats should reach an internal temperature of at least 152°F. Higher internal temperatures are safe, but the meat may be excessively dry. Flavor and tenderness are enhanced by a low cooking temperature of 160°F or slightly more. Many smokers have a heat indicator that says too cold, too hot, or just right. Precise cooking temperatures are difficult, to say the least, with this type of indicator. To ensure a safe and thoroughly cooked product, a meat thermometer is a worthwhile investment. Cooking at these low temperatures is a time consuming process, often 10 hours or more for a brisket or turkey. Chicken pieces may take only 3 to 4 hours. Fish fillets take even less time. The process can be speeded up by higher temperatures, but quality may suffer. I usually cook my items at about 180°F.

Curing Meats

Pork and other meats are often cured with a curing agent prior to smoking. Curing agents typically contain a small amount of sodium nitrite on a salt carrier. The sodium nitrite acts as a preservative of sorts, in addition to its other properties. The art and science of curing meats is outside the scope of this book.

Process

The process is simple, and about the same for all meats. Place the meats on racks, fill any water pans, add wood or herbs to the burning tray/container, and you're off. As earlier noted, the meats should be marinated ahead of time. I like to turn the meats one time to provide more even browning.

Other Things Worth Noting

It only takes about 30 minutes for wood smoke and herb smoke to flavor your cooking. If using a water smoker, watch your water level. Allow enough time, but don't overcook either. Meats and other things can dry out, even in a water smoker.

...But I Don't Have A Smoker

All is not lost! You can use your plain ole oven- be it electric or gas. Add about one teaspoon liquid smoke to your marinade. It's not like the real thing, but it's close. Follow the same procedure, except cook the meat in your oven at about 180-190 degrees F for about the same amount of time listed for a smoker. Use a pan (the pan to your broiler works OK). Cover with foil for all but the last hour in the oven. Remember your meat thermometer.

<u>Charcoal Broiling</u>

Steaks and hamburgers. Cooking steaks, hamburgers, and other foods outside on a charcoal grill has been one of man's fancies for a long time. Charcoal or flame broiling imparts a unique flavor to some of our favorite foods. Although a charcoal broiled steak tastes good, a marinated charcoal broiled steak tastes better. Of course, that's just my opinion. Let some good steaks soak in my beef marinade (next page) for a while before they're placed on the grill. The same goes for hamburger patties. After applying the marinade, charcoal like you've been doing. Your method is probably as good as mine. Re-marinate the meat occasionally while cooking.

Chicken. Chickens by the half or by the piece also taste better if they've spent some time in the marinade pot. I find it best to cook chicken via indirect heat. In other words, place charcoal to both sides of the chicken, but none under it. This works especially well if the grill has a cover. Also, work some spices under the chicken skin before broiling.

Flavoring with wood smoke. While charcoal adds flavor, a few small chunks of smoker wood on top of the charcoal adds more flavor. First, soak your favorite flavor of wood (i.e. pecan) in water for a few minutes. Place one or two pieces on top the charcoal, then watch the smoke begin its magic.

Marinades

Successful smokery cooking requires a good marinade. After completing the marinade, place the meat and marinade in a plastic zipper bag, and let the two commingle in the refrigerator over night, if possible - or at least 4 hours. Turn the bag at least once.

Marinades provide both flavor and tenderizing. Wine is a specified ingredient in my marinades. If you are a non-wine user, substitute white grape juice or red/purple grape juice respectively.

Beef Marinade

Ingredients

1. ¼ cup vegetable oil
2. ¼ cup red wine (Port, etc.)
3. ¼ cup soy sauce
4. 3 Tbs. Worcestershire sauce
5. 2 Tbs. raspberry vinegar or wine vinegar
6. 1 Tbs. dry mustard
7. 2 tsp. *Rice's Beef Enhancer™*
8. ¼ cup honey and molasses, mixed
9. 3 cloves garlic
10. 1 tsp. sized piece of ginger root

Place all ingredients in a blender and process for about 1-2 minutes. Makes enough marinade for an 8-10 pound brisket. Also enough for a big bunch of steaks. Freeze any excess for future use.

Pork Marinade

Follow the above recipe except use white wine or sherry and *Rice's Pork Enhancer™* - page 21.

"How can one dog eat a whole smoked brisket? Ask mine to find out."

Chicken Marinade

Ingredients

1. ¼ cup vegetable oil
2. ¼ cup sherry or white wine
3. ¼ cup light soy sauce
4. 3 Tbs. Worcestershire sauce
5. 2 Tbs. raspberry vinegar or wine vinegar
6. 1 Tbs. dry mustard
7. 1 tsp. *Rice's Chicken Enhancer™*
8. ¼ cup honey
9. 2 cloves garlic
10. 1 tsp. ginger root

Place all ingredients in a blender and process for 1-2 minutes. Enough marinade for 3 chickens, so you might want to halve the recipe. Marinades freeze well.

Seafood Marinade

1. ¼ cup olive oil (vegetable oil can be substituted)
2. ¼ cup sherry or white wine
3. 1 Tbs. light soy sauce
4. 2 Tbs. white wine vinegar
5. 1 tsp. dry mustard
6. 1 tsp. *Rice's Seafood Enhancer™*
7. ½ tsp. horseradish
8. 1 tsp. sugar
9. 1 clove garlic

Place all ingredients in a blender and process for 1-2 minutes. Makes enough marinade for about 2 pounds of seafood.

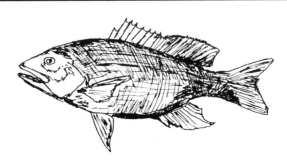

Notes

Chapter 11

Margaret's Recipes

A Man's fancy often turns to other things besides cooking, thank goodness. There's love, marriage, kids, puppies, a home, and a mortgage -- just to name a few. When a man's fancy turns to the fairer sex, other cooking ideas and techniques are just a few of the benefits. Margaret and I grew up in the same town-- Amarillo, Texas. We attended different grade schools and junior high schools; I guess they're called middle schools now. We both attended the only high school that existed in Amarillo then. Ours was the last senior class in Amarillo to graduate from a single high school. Palo Duro High also graduated a class the following year. If you're a good detective, you can find out what year that was. Palo Duro and two other high schools are now present in Amarillo. Our old alma mater, Amarillo High, was destroyed by fire several years ago. Time changes lots of things.

We got to know each other later at Amarillo College. I guess our paths didn't cross at Amarillo High. Later after I graduated from Texas Tech University and Margaret captured a teaching degree from West Texas State University, our courtship began. I remember our first picnic with fried chicken, cooked by Margaret, of course. Then there was the trip to Lake McClellan, where our day and picnic was interrupted by a foraging Billy goat. Didn't know a little ole Billy goat could cause such a stir. I thought he was kind of cute -- but Margaret thought otherwise.

I remember hearing about creamed chipped beef for lunch. What was creamed chipped beef? It must have been something fancy! Actually, upon my first invitation to lunch, I discovered it was actually dried beef in a white sauce. A new name if not a new taste. Then there were the trout that I proudly brought back from New Mexico. They were cleaned to the nth degree. I later found that they were turned over to my future father-in-law. Margaret was scared to death of fish bones.

With our marriage came some new adventures in the cooking world. Our families cooking styles were different. Margaret's dad was a master at burnt toast, but to my knowledge never fired up a charcoal grill. I guess his fancy never turned to cooking --

only golf. Margaret and her mother were the cooks of the family. I remember their rump roast and the fixin's, including cherry pie. Both her family and mine were turkey people during the holidays.

Margaret feels that the superb cook of her family was her paternal grandmother. Margaret's tales of trips to Oklahoma City to the grandparent's acreage brought pleasure to both of us. A big garden provided fresh fruits and vegetables - potatoes and more. And I thought men were supposed to be the meat and potato lovers of the world. Margaret talked of the superb cakes, pies, and cookies stirred up without a recipe. How in the world did Margaret weigh in at under a hundred pounds when we were married?

There are a few unique dishes that were handed down through her family that she has offered to share in this book. According to our genealogical searches, the recipes originated on the Isle of Åland, between Finland and Sweden. I remember these dishes well. Both the kids and I thought they were very good. Find something that kids will eat beside French fries, and you've got something worth sharing.

Margaret's Rump Roast

Ingredients

1. Rump roast -- fresh or thawed
2. Garlic clove
3. 1 Tbs. Worcestershire sauce
4. Pepper
5. 1 tsp. vegetable oil
6. ½ cup water
7. 2 Tbs. flour for gravy
8. ½ cup water

Heat a pot over high heat until a drop of water sizzles. Add oil, and coat the pot's bottom. Yes, you will have lots of smoke both now and later, so turn on the vent. Put garlic in a garlic press and rub over the roast. Sprinkle pepper over the roast. Brown the roast on all sides thoroughly (very important). Add ½ cup water and Worcestershire sauce. Reduce heat to low, and cook covered until tender - about 3 hours. Add water along the way if necessary to keep from boiling dry.

What's a roast without **gravy!** Remove the roast to a serving platter. Add water if necessary to yield about two cups of liquid. Adjust heat to medium-low. Shake the flour and the ½ cup of water together in a covered container until the mixture is smooth and lump free; if you're an expert you can stir flour into the ½ cup water. Add flour mixture to the liquid in the pot and stir quickly to avoid lumps. Remove from heat when thickened.

Cut the roast into thin slices and serve with gravy, and of course mashed potatoes. The roast will slice more easily after it cools while the gravy is being prepared. I like a little horseradish sauce with my roast beef, but Margaret takes hers straight.

Roast beef hash. The main reason to have rump roast is so that hash can be made with the leftovers. Chop the leftover roast, two or 3 pared potatoes, and one medium peeled onion in a food processor until the mixture is pea sized. Brown in oil and cook for about 10-15 minutes, turning two or three times.

> "The main reason to have rump roast is so that hash can be made with the leftovers."

A Peek At Scandinavian Foods

My mind had visualized a Norwegian breakfast table long before I ever saw one. There was hot bread, a few eggs, maybe fish of some sort, etc. One thing I was sure of was that breakfast would be hot. What else would one expect in a country so cold? My first visit proved how wrong a visualization can be. Breakfast table fare is usually coo-oold. Cold bread, umpteen kinds of cold herring, cold boiled eggs, cold cheese, cold everything. Denmark and Sweden, at least on my visits, resembled my visualization a teeny bit closer. At least a little warm food adorned the table.

I visualized Norway and seafood in the same picture. This image was pretty true to form. The fish soup at *Jan's* (a restaurant in Stavanger) was excellent. It consisted of a superb stock which a local resident said was made by boiling fish heads --eyes and all. It had salmon, mussels, krabbe (crab), reker (shrimp), and other tasty morsels. *Jan's* also served monkfish, an ugly monster looking affair, with unique textured fillets. It was quite tasty. Reindeer was on the menu, along with cloudberries, and other unusual items.

Fresh vegetables were plentiful in the farmers' markets during Norway's brief summer. Most were of the cabbage or root family. Lots of Brussels sprouts, cabbages, cauliflower, carrots, etc. Selections were very limited in winter. A Napa type cabbage was a prime ingredient for salads in winter. Somehow it looked pretty awful by the time spring arrived. I've mentioned Norway's tiny potatoes. They are, at least compared with our Idaho russets.

Cows in Norway were made for milking, rather than for table beef. Tough, sure enough! A common tale was that chickens for the market were killed by starvation. Pretty tough and stringy individuals, if you ask me. Danish chickens, if you could find them, were much better. I don't recall seeing a single pig during my stay. So much for local bacon, but imported bacon and ham were readily available. Lamb was a staple in the meat department.

I remember the cream and pastry desserts though. They were something to brag about. Perhaps the biggest craving that I had during my Norway venture was for a good old-fashioned American hamburger. Now you know why my first stop in America was at the Whataburger® Store.

Swedish Stuffed Cabbage

We called these things cabbage rollups.

Ingredients

1. 8 large cabbage leaves
2. 1 pound ground beef
3. 2 Tbs. rice
4. 3/4 cup milk
5. 2 Tbs. bacon fat (or oil)
6. ½ cup bouillon
7. ½ cup milk
8. ½ tsp. salt
9. Pepper - nutmeg to taste, about ¼ tsp. of each.

Parboil cabbage leaves for about 10 minutes. Cook rice in 3/4 cup milk until tender. Combine ground beef, rice, salt, pepper, and nutmeg. Place meat mixture evenly divided on the cabbage leaves, and fold the leaves to retain the mixture. Brown the rolled leaves in oil or bacon fat, and remove to a baking dish. Add ½ cup milk and bouillon to the baking dish and bake at 375°F for about an hour.

Swedish Pancakes

Our kids favorite!

Ingredients

1. 2 large eggs
2. ½ cup flour
3. ½ tsp. salt
4. 2 tsp. butter or margarine, melted
5. 1 tsp. sugar
6. 1½ cups milk

Mix ingredients 1-5 with ½ cup of the milk, stirring vigorously. Add remaining milk slowly while continuing to stir the mixture. Use a special pancake cooker, or cooked in a shallow skillet that has been sprayed with cooking oil. Makes about half enough for three hungry sons and daughters.

Kruhkräkers

Scandinavian dumpling dishes are somewhat unique. In Norway, I remember komelar (pronounced koom-la). This "corned" lamb stew was adorned with the world's heaviest (in my opinion) potato dumplings. I often remarked that if lead weights and komelar dumplings were simultaneously sent to the bottom of the deepest fjord, the dumplings would arrive first. Swedish kruhkräkers are somewhat lighter fare, and make a unique meal. This recipe was relayed in a letter to Margaret's mother from Margaret's paternal grandmother.

Ingredients:

1. 1 pound lean pork shoulder, ground (or other ground meat)
2. ½ tsp. salt
3. 1 medium onion, finely chopped
4. 3 cooked potatoes; mashed without milk; kept warm
5. 6 raw grated potatoes
6. 2 cups flour
7. 3 quarts of water
8. 1 cup flour to be added if needed
9. 1 cup milk
10. ½ tsp. salt

Kruhkräkers, Continued

Assembly:

1. Mix items 1-3 thoroughly, and cook in a covered pan until well done. Do not brown. Refrigerate for at least an hour. When the mixture is cooled and congealed, form into balls approximately 1 inch in diameter. My son forms one inch meatballs from the raw products and boils them in the water (item 7) over low heat until well done (about 20 minutes). Either option yields about the same result. Set aside in a cool place.

2. While the mashed potatoes are still warm, add the flour (item 6). Stir the mixture to form a dough. Shred/grate the first potato. Pat the grated potato to remove what water you can. Stir into the dough. Repeat for the remainder of the potatoes (item 5). The dough will be stiff. Rinse hands in cold water so that the potato mixture doesn't stick to them. Make a dough patty in the palm of your hand. place a meatball in the center of the patty. Form a potato covering around each meat ball, using care to ensure that the meat is fully covered. The thinner the dough, the better the result. As the dough stands, it will become more moist. Add some of the reserve flour (item 8) if necessary.

3. Boil water and salt (item 10) in a large pot. Lower dumplings one at a time slowly into boiling water, and cook 20 minutes after the last dumpling has been added. Dumplings should not be stacked. Dumplings may stick to the bottom of the pot. If so, carefully lift dumplings so that they will rise to the top. Depending on pot size, two or more batches may be necessary. Cook second batch in the same liquid. Remove dumplings to a serving bowl or platter. Add any remaining meat mixture to the liquid. Add milk, reheat, and serve with dumplings.

Makes 4-6 servings; 10-12 dumplings.

Adaptations

The above recipe includes the original ingredients and process --at least as we interpreted the recipe. Using my creative license, I substituted chicken broth for about half the water. I also added ½ tsp. *Rice's Pork Enhancer* ™ (page 21) to the meat mixture.

The German Dish

I'm sure that there must be a fancier name for this, but we don't know what it is.

Ingredients

1. 1 round steak, tenderized
2. 1 small onion, about ½ cup
3. ½ cup dill pickles
4. 1 Tbs. fat or oil.

Cut round steak into about 6-8 pieces. Use a meat mallet to flatten the pieces to about ¼ inch thickness. Chop the onions and pickles together in a food processor, or by hand until they reach a coarse meal-like texture. Spread the onion-pickle mixture evenly distributed among the meat pieces. Roll the meat pieces into cylinders and secure with tooth picks. Brown in fat over high heat and cook covered over low heat until tender; about an hour.

Chapter 12

<u>Holiday Tradition</u>

Holidays are for cooking! Except for the first warm days of spring when the barbecue bug bites, nothing stirs my cooking instinct more than Thanksgiving and Christmas. Perhaps, nothing else lives so vividly in one's memories. I can remember my first Christmas turkey vividly.   Margaret's mom and dad spent Christmas at our home for the first time. Up till then, Christmas was spent at the homes of our parents, brothers, and sisters. Being the youngest of the children in my family, visiting my sisters was like being home.

Mother-in-law Helen looked dubious when Margaret told her that we (Margaret and I) were doing Christmas dinner. Her only advice was, "start early in the morning. An eighteen pound turkey takes a while to cook." Father-in-law Cliff purchased his usual turkey for us. He liked big Tom turkeys.

We were up at 5:00 AM. Of course, the kids saw to that - turkey or no turkey. I had prepared the onions, celery, and bread cubes the night before. Margaret had baked a batch of cornbread also for the stuffing. We assembled the stuffing in just a few minutes Christmas morning -- dodging forages by the kids with the stuff Santa had brought. You see, Helen didn't know that I was an old hand at this cooking the fowl business. Years of duck and goose hunting had taught me something. That big Tom turkey was stuffed and in the oven well before 6:00 AM. Helen had this outstanding shocked look on her face when the turkey came out, cooked to a tee, a little after 11:00 AM. Dinner was on the table at 12:00 noon sharp! Since then, at least 70 turkeys have proceeded in and out of our ovens, although not all of them were ready at 12:00 noon sharp.

Margaret and I will be the dubious ones when our kids do that first turkey, and we can retire from the turkey business. Somehow though, I can't see my daughters or sons-in-law up at 5:00 AM, wrestling an eighteen pound turkey. At least my taste for turkey is something a little smaller- say, fourteen pounds. Following are a few tricks that I've learned about the turkey business. An experience base of more than seventy turkeys should at least qualify me as an apprentice guru or something.

Christmas and Thanksgiving Dinner

Margaret and I have always thought turkey was the only game in town for these special holidays. We hosted a southern Christmas one year in Houston. About 25 family members attended. As I remember, we also had ham for that special holiday.

Our Typical Menu

- **Waldorf Salad**
- **Baked Oysters - Sometimes**
- **Roast Turkey and Stuffing**
- **Mashed Potatoes**
- **Gravy with Giblets**
- **Hot Bread or Rolls**
- **Fresh Cranberry Sauce**
- **Pecan Pie**
- **Pumpkin Pie**
- **Broccoli or Other Green Veggie**

A few times, we've added another thing or two -- for example, yams, apple pie, and more. Our daughter, Cheryl and her husband, Everett have also provided a broccoli casserole from time to time. The other traditional menu items are always on the table. The holidays wouldn't be the same without them.

Christmas eve in our home is the time for snacks and *hors d'oeuvres*. Menu items usually include: smoked cocktail sausages with barbecue sauce, a pecan-cheese log, fruit and a dip made from cream cheese and marshmallow cream, Swedish or other meatballs, raw vegetables and dip, blackened shrimp with barbecue sauce, queso and tortilla chips, and an occasional new item from time to time. Sweets might include cookies, brownies, pecan pralines, and other homemade candies.

Waldorf Salad

Waldorf salad is often the first thing on the table, so I'll list it first. I'm not sure where this recipe originated. We stir up our version without reference to a written recipe.

Ingredients:

1. 3 medium tart apples such as: Granny Smith, Winesap, Fuji.
2. ½ cup chopped pecans, toasted 15 minutes at 300°F.
3. 2 stalks celery, coarsely chopped.
4. ¼ cup Miracle Whip® salad dressing.
5. Sugar or sweetener to taste.
6. ¼ tsp. salt.
7. 1 Tbs. lemon juice.
8. 1-2 cups small marshmallows (the kids like 2 cups or more).

Prepare the dressing by mixing items 4-7 together. We pare our apples, but the peelings can be left on if you prefer. Cube the apples into bite-sized pieces. Place them in the dressing, and stir thoroughly so that the apples won't turn brown. Add chopped celery and nuts. Stir in marshmallows just before serving. Makes about 6 servings.

Baked Oysters

Ingredients

1. Oysters, fresh or canned -- about 12 - 16 ounces.
2. Crackers -- about half a box.
3. Butter or margarine -- about 2 Tbs.
4. Milk.

This is another one of Margaret's measureless recipes. Drain the oysters. Crumble enough crackers to cover the bottom of a medium baking dish. Add about 1/3 of the oysters, distributed over the crackers. Dot with butter. Repeat layers of crackers, oysters, and butter, ending with crackers/butter. Pour enough milk into the mixture to thoroughly moisten. Bake at 350 degrees for about 35 minutes. Serves about 6, or 8, or 10, depending on who likes oysters.

Turkey and Stuffing

This is the main course for our traditional holiday dinner. A good version can make your day; a bad version can also make your day ......miserable. A key is a good turkey. I like a self basting version with a built in doneness indicator. After years of testing, Honeysuckle White® has yielded my best results. Perhaps one common problem is overcooking; take the turkey out of the oven when the indicator first pops. How did that turkey get into the oven in the first place? Here are step by step instructions.

1. If you don't have a covered turkey roaster, consider buying one. It makes the turkey ordeal much easier. Otherwise, use a large roasting pan and cover the bird with heavy foil; seal the foil to the pan's rim.

2. If using a frozen bird, allow plenty of time to thaw. Follow directions on the turkey.

3. After thawing, unwrap the turkey, then remove the neck and giblet packages. They are usually in the bird's body and neck cavity, respectively. It may be a trick to pry the legs out of the wire retainer. I use a screwdriver after I once broke a perfectly good knife.

4. Rinse the giblets and neck in cold water. I've always wondered how my turkeys ever lived without a liver. About half the time, my turkey's liver is missing, and we like turkey liver in our giblet gravy. Turkeys also have small hearts or no hearts. Well, so much for turkey anatomy. Place the neck and what giblets you have in a large saucepan, add plenty of water, and simmer over low heat until the turkey in the oven is done. Add water, if necessary, along the way.

5. Rinse the turkey with cold water, or soak in cold salt water for an hour if you have time. Drain the turkey as well as you can.

6. I like to stuff my turkey with dressing. You can, of course, cook the stuffing separately. Form loose balls of stuffing in your hand, and start filling the body cavity. Lace the cavity shut with skewers and string. Do the same for the neck cavity. I put regular bread stuffing in the body cavity, and pecan stuffing in the neck cavity.

7. Roast according to directions on the turkey. Use care not to overcook or undercook. Save the roaster drippings for giblet gravy.

Bread Stuffing with Pecans

Stuffing or dressing? Either name means the same in my book. Some like pecans in their stuffing; others don't. I do some of each. Adjust the proportions for a larger turkey. Cook the extra stuffing separately for a smaller turkey.

Ingredients for a 14 Pound Turkey

1. 1¼ cups butter or margarine (2½ sticks)
2. 2 cups celery with leaves, chopped
3. 1 cup onions, chopped
4. 1 box "JIFFY" Cornbread- baked using directions on the box.
5. 8 cups bread cubes, crust removed
6. 2 tsp. salt
7. ½ tsp. pepper
8. 2 tsp. rubbed or powdered sage
9. 1 tsp. *Rice's Chicken Enhancer™*
10. ½ cup chopped pecans (optional)

Sauté the onions and celery in melted butter until the onion turns translucent. Add enough of the bread cubes to absorb most of the butter. Pour the mixture from the pan into a large mixing container. I use the top of the turkey roaster. Crumble cornbread, and stir into the mixture. Add the remaining ingredients and mix thoroughly. I place the pecans in about half the stuffing, leaving the rest for the plain stuffing fanciers. Stuff your bird, or cook in a baking dish for about an hour. Depending on the moisture content of the bread, a little turkey or chicken broth may be necessary for a good consistency. Stuffing should form a loose ball in your hands, without excessive crumbling. Add an additional half cup liquid if the stuffing is to be cooked outside the turkey. Makes enough for an average 14 pound turkey with a little left over. Some 14 pound turkeys have more room for stuffing than others.

Giblet Gravy

Remove neck and giblets to a plate for cooling. Pour the giblet liquid through a strainer into the roaster drippings. Place about ¼ cup flour and cup of water into a container with a lid. Shake vigorously. Heat the turkey liquids, and gradually stir in the flour mixture. Cook until the mixture thickens. Chop the neck meat and giblets into small pieces, and add to the gravy. Depending on the amount of liquid, additional flour may be necessary to yield a consistency that you like.

Other Menu Items

- Pecan pie - see page 103.
- Pumpkin pie: Use the recipe on the "**Libby's**" label, with the crust on page 103.
- Buy fresh cranberries and prepare according to the package directions.
- Use your bread machine like I do, or buy some rolls.
- Steam the broccoli until crisp-tender.
- Mash the potatoes as you always do.

That Turkey Carcass --Yuk!

Of all the holiday jobs, I am blessed with the worst one of all - disposing of the turkey remains. Everybody likes the white meat, so the carcass usually has a fair amount of the unwhite meat left clinging to the bones. I use my hands and a sharp knife to remove all the meat that I can.

Now, it's just me and our dog Katie in the kitchen. Everybody else has somehow disappeared. Oh, the cat was there for a minute until Katie's bark sent her to the top of the refrigerator. Katie tolerates absolutely no catly interference during turkey time. Somehow, de-meating a turkey always results in a morsel or two headed towards the floor. Katie's superior eye to mouth coordination never lets them complete their journey. Katie also ends up with a little of the other stuff too. She received her Ph.D. in begging a long time ago.

After disjointing the leg and wing bones, I rinse the back in water to get rid of the stuffing remnants. Then, I toss it all into a stock pot with a little celery and onion, and of course, water. These turkey remains make excellent stock, and there's no such thing as too much chicken/turkey stock.

What about all that unwhite meat?

Use it in place of chicken in NuMex, and other recipes. Turkey and chicken simulate each other pretty well. Turkey hash is also a pretty good way to go. See the recipe on page 119. One of our favorite uses is for turkey croquettes. These things are hard to find in a cookbook, so I'll list the recipe here.

Turkey Croquettes

Ingredients

1. 2 cups shredded turkey (use food processor with metal blade)
2. 1 Tbs. onion, finely chopped
3. 1 recipe thick white sauce, see below
4. ¼ tsp. each: paprika, salt, pepper
5. Dash of nutmeg
6. 2 tsp. lemon juice
7. 1 Tbs. chopped cilantro or parsley
8. 1 egg plus 2 Tbs. water, slightly beaten
9. Breadcrumbs

Mix ingredients 1-7 thoroughly. Wet your hands, then form the mixture into balls about an inch in diameter. Dip the balls into the egg mixture, then cover with breadcrumbs. Roll between your hands to form cones, or leave in the original ball shape. Fry in deep oil for about 3 minutes. Serves 4 or 5 .

Thick White Sauce

1. ¼ cup margarine or butter
2. ¼ cup flour
3. ¼ tsp. salt
4. ¼ tsp. pepper
5. 1 cup milk

Melt butter. Over low heat, add flour, salt, pepper, to make a bubbling paste. Stir in milk gradually. Stir constantly to avoid sticking. White sauce loves to scorch on the bottom of the pan. Continue until mixture thickens and starts to bubble.

That's All, Folks

All good things must come to an end, as the saying goes. All bad things must come to an end -- or so we hope. Hopefully, this book will be classified as a good thing. It covers some of the many things that I've learned about cooking for over a half-century. Gee, that sounds like a long time, doesn't it.

It seems that the more you know about cooking and lots of other things, the less you understand. For example, my grandsons would rather eat a hot dog than the best marinated beef T-bone steak. They don't like mustard; they love catsup. They think all those wonderful aromatic herbs smell yucky. They refuse to eat tacos if one teeny little piece of lettuce gets in the shell some way or another. Even Katie, the dog, eats her tacos with lettuce!

I've dabbled in many cooking styles that aren't covered in this book. Some cookery skills seem to be beyond my capabilities. For example, there's chicken fried steak. I just can't seem to master chicken fried steak! Oh, my steaks are about as good as some that I've seen advertised, *"Best chicken fried steak in the country."* All I can say is that it was evidently a small country. The best chicken fried steak that I've ever eaten was in a Wheeler, Texas, restaurant.

Oriental cuisine is another of my favorites. I'd go to a Chinese restaurant 3 times a week if Margaret would let me. I'll admit that I've tried my hand at Chinese cooking a few times. Tasted pretty good, I'll have to admit. But talk about a mess! I was about ready to throw myself out of my own kitchen. Talk about time consuming! I thought I would starve to death before it was ready. Then there's the technology of folding won-ton. How could something so easy be so complex? For Chinese and Thai cooking, follow my advice and find a good restaurant. Maybe that's why we eat out a lot, in spite of the fact that I'm a cook-book author. Before the kids left the nest though, we did cook most of our meals at home.

So, good foods are in the eyes of the beholder. The best can be made better. The superior can be made more superior -- if you bend Webster's definitions just a little. Making that special recipe better can be lots of fun -- both in the doing and in the eating. That's how it is with cooking!

Index

Asparagus 46

Beans
Bean soup 69
Bean enhancer 22
Frijoles charros 73

Beef
Beef filling 89
Beef stock 27
Beef marinade 114
Beef steak with pickles 124
Beef enhancer 21
Beefy vegetable soup 66
Fruity meat tacos 96

Black cherries 54
Black walnuts 43-44

Blackberries
Blackberries 1, 49
Blackberries-wild 149
Blackberry cobbler 50

Blossoms-elderberry 53
Bob's Pancakes 62
Bread stuffing with pecans 129
Brisket-smoked 8
Broth-turkey 130
Brownies-pecan double fudge 107
Cabbage-stuffed 121
Caramel custard 98
Carcass-turkey 130
Cheese and onion filling 90
Cheesy broccoli soup 68
Cherries-wild 54
Cilantro 81

Chicken
Chicken-barbecued 113
Chicken and dumplings 56

Chicken-continued
Chicken and noodles 56
Chicken enhancer 21
Chicken filling-NuMex 90
Chicken marinade 115
Chicken-marinated fried 57
Chicken-smoked 112-113
Chicken stock 26

Chiles
Chiles 79-87
Chiles-types 78
Chiles rellenos 102
Chiles-roasted 6, 79

Chili
Chili 60-61
Chili-red herbal 61
Chili-white herbal 60

Cookies
Choco-nutaholic cookies 100

Chokecherries 54
Chokecherry jelly 54
Christmas foods 125-132
Cobbler-blackberry 50
Corn tortillas 94
Croquettes-turkey 131
Cumin 81

Desserts
Blackberry cobbler 50
Choco-nutaholic cookies 100
Elderberry blossoms-fried 53
Flan 98
Honey pecan pie 103
Pecan nougat bars 104
Pecan yummy bars 105
Pecan fudge brownies 107

133
